USMC M4A2 SHERMAN
VS
JAPANESE TYPE 95 HA-GO

Central Pacific 1943–44

ROMAIN CANSIÈRE in collaboration with Ed Gilbert

OSPREY PUBLISHING
Bloomsbury Publishing Plc
PO Box 883, Oxford, OX1 9PL, UK
1385 Broadway, 5th Floor, New York, NY 10018, USA
E-mail: info@ospreypublishing.com
www.ospreypublishing.com

OSPREY is a trademark of Osprey Publishing Ltd

First published in Great Britain in 2021

A catalog record for this book is available from the British Library.

ISBN: PB 9781472840110; eBook 9781472840127; ePDF 9781472840097;
XML 9781472840103

21 22 23 24 25   10 9 8 7 6 5 4 3 2 1

Artwork by Edouard Groult
Map by Bounford.com
Index by Angela Hall
Typeset by PDQ Digital Media Solutions, Bungay, UK
Printed and bound in India by Replika Press Private Ltd.

Artist's note

Readers can find out more about Edouard Groult's work by visiting the
following website:
https://www.artstation.com/edwardca

Osprey Publishing supports the Woodland Trust, the UK's leading woodland
conservation charity.

To find out more about our authors and books visit
www.ospreypublishing.com. Here you will find extracts, author interviews,
details of forthcoming events, and the option to sign up for our newsletter.

Acknowledgments

First of all, we would like to acknowledge the veterans who shared their
personal experience with us, namely Edward L. Bale Jr, Michael Shivetts, Joe
D. Woolum, Robert Meier, Robert U. Falkenbury and Philip C. Morell.
Special thanks go to Oliver Barnham who bought and restored a late model of
Type 95 and kindly allowed us to inspect his Ha-Go and shared many
technical documents and photographs. Akira Takizawa provided information
on Japanese tank unit organization and technical data on the Ha-Go. He also
allowed us to use the translation of Shiro Shimoda's account, published in his
book *World War II Japanese Tank Tactics*. Pierre Olivier Buand provided
technical advice on the Sherman tank.
As usual, the Marine Corps History Division (MCHD), particularly Alisa
Whitley and Annette Amerman, the US National Archives (NARA) and the
National Museum of the Pacific War (NMPW) staff were highly instrumental
in locating photographs and documents.
Jonathan Holt, archivist at the Bovington Tank Museum's Archives (UK)
helped with locating reports and photographs on the Type 95.
Kenneth W. Estes provided photographs as well as help regarding the early use
of tanks by the Marine Corps. Morgan Gillard, Kirby Nave and Mark and
Porfirio G. "PG" Navarro provided photographs.
Thanks to Vera Verchinina and Gauthier Delaforge for the translation of the
Russian report on the Ha-Go (see bibliography).
James Mason and Robert Moore provided precious help in locating and
organizing veterans' interviews.
Last but not least, we would like to acknowledge the on-site research assistance
provided by Caroline Cansière and Catherine R. Gilbert. Catherine R. Gilbert
and Nikolai Bogdanovic edited the manuscript.
I, Romain, am indebted to my co-author and friend Ed for his trust, help and
guidance over the past years, during which we cooperated on many projects.
Ed's altruism and father-like attitude taught me a lot, not only about the
Marines Corps. This is one of two posthumously published books by Ed.

Dedication

To the American and Japanese tankers of the Great Pacific War.

Abbreviations

AP	armor piercing
APC	armor-piercing capped ammunition
APHE	Armor Piercing High-Explosive
CINCPAC	Commander-in-chief, US Pacific Fleet
CINCPOA	Commander-in-chief, Pacific Ocean Areas
H&S	Headquarters and Service
IJA	Imperial Japanese Army
IJN	Imperial Japanese Navy
IMB	Independent Mixed Brigade
LCM	Landing Craft Mechanized
LCVP	Landing Craft Vehicle Personnel
LSD	Landing Ship Dock
LVT	Landing Vehicle Tracked
PTO	Pacific Theater of Operations
SNLF	Special Naval Landing Forces
SPM	self-propelled mount
USMC	United States Marine Corps

Photographic sources

MCHD	Marine Corps History Division
NARA	National Archives and Records Administration
NMPW	National Museum of the Pacific War

Editor's note

In most cases imperial measurements have been used in this book. For ease of
comparison please refer to the following conversion table:

1 NM = 1.85km
1yd = 0.9m
1ft = 0.3m
1in. = 2.54cm/25.4mm
1kn = 1.85km/h
1 long ton = 1.02 metric tonnes
1lb = 0.45kg

Front cover, above: M4A2 Sherman Bonita. (Edouard Groult)
Front cover, below: Type 95 Ha-Go. (Edouard Groult)

CONTENTS

INTRODUCTION

When the Japanese air and naval forces attacked the American fleet at Pearl Harbor on December 7, 1941, Japan had been at war since 1931. Experience gained in the battles fought against China led the Japanese to modernize their weapons. The thriving Japanese war economy allowed for the development of a new light tank: the Type 95 Ha-Go, armed with a 37mm main gun. It made its combat debut in China in 1936. It would become the most produced tank the Japanese built during the war.

America was unprepared for war: its army ranked nineteenth in terms of size, behind Portugal. At the end of World War I, the US Army generals decided the US Marine Corps had no part in a future war in Europe. Since then, the Marine Corps had struggled to survive budget and manpower restrictions. In tandem with the US Navy, it began to specialize in amphibious warfare in anticipation of an eventual war in the Pacific against Japan.

The US doctrine of the early war period provided a number of antitank guns and tank destroyers (called self-propelled mounts—SPMs—by the Marines) within infantry regiments to deal with enemy tanks. Here, a 1st Marine Division M2 SPM is landing at Cape Gloucester in December 1944. (MCHD)

When the war broke out, Navy and Marine Corps staffs were caught out before a tank light enough to be carried ashore in a landing craft had been successfully developed. Unsatisfactory test results of current prototypes and lack of time forced the Marines to fall back on existing Army-designed light tanks. However, the American entry into the war boosted research, and by 1942, the Sherman, a medium tank equipped with a 75mm main gun, rolled off the production lines. In company with the development of the new tank, the US also developed a new landing craft that could carry the new 32-ton Sherman. However, the Marines would

The Japanese relied on suicide teams, mines, and antitank guns to knock out enemy armor. Here on Saipan, a 100lb bomb has been converted into an improvised explosive device. Fortunately for the crew of A-30 Amapola, only the antitank mine positioned atop the bomb—used as the detonator—exploded. (NARA)

have to wait until 1943 before being equipped with the first batch of M4A2s, the diesel version of the Sherman tank. Like the Japanese Ha-Go, the Sherman would become the most-produced American tank of the war.

The war in the Pacific has been extensively documented from the infantry perspective for obvious reasons. The infantry was the spearhead of both the American drive through the Pacific and the Japanese defense. Both sides knew that the small islands captured by the Americans would serve as sea- or airbases for the ultimate operation, an all-out assault on the Japanese homeland.

Both the US Marines and the Japanese used tanks to provide direct infantry support in the field. Given the nature of the conflict in the Central Pacific, American and Japanese tank crews primarily trained to reduce fortifications or counterattack enemy beachheads as opposed to fighting other tanks. Both sides had weapons and doctrines specially designed to defeat enemy tanks.

Japanese antitank doctrine leaned on suicide teams, mines, and antitank guns to destroy enemy tanks. Likewise, the US Marines' antitank doctrine was based on infantry-manned weapons such as bazookas, 37mm antitank guns, or tank destroyers (half-tracks mounting a 75mm gun) also known as self-propelled mounts (SPMs).

However, Japanese and US Marine tanks did face each other in a series of small but brutal skirmishes during the American Central Pacific drive in 1943 and 1944.

This work will describe the duels that occurred between the most commonly used tanks of the Pacific War: the Japanese light tank Type 95 Ha-Go and the Marine Corps medium tank M4A2 Sherman.

The technical disparity between the Sherman and the Ha-Go left little doubt as to the result of an encounter between these tanks. The outcome of these duels was usually the same: destruction of the Japanese tank. Despite the Sherman's great technical superiority—some historians have characterized the M4 as the "Tiger of the Pacific" (in reference to the famous German heavy tank of World War II)—the Japanese tank crews' tenacity gave the Marine tankers great difficulty.

CHRONOLOGY

1931

September 18   Invasion of Manchuria by Japanese forces.

1934

The Type 95 Ha-Go development program begins.

1940s

The US Army starts the medium tank program.

1941

February   Development of the M4 medium tank.

December 7–8   Beginning of the Pacific War.
December 22   First tank-on-tank battle involving American M3 and Japanese Type 95 tanks in the Philippines. The Ha-Gos are victorious.

1943

January   The USMC obtains its first M4A2s.
November 20   First tank-versus-tank battle involving a USMC M4A2 and a Type 95 during the Battle of Tarawa.

1944

February 18 and 22   M4A2s supporting the 22nd Marines destroy six Ha-Gos during the battle for Eniwetok Atoll.
June 15 to July 9   Battle of Saipan. The night of June 16/17, the Japanese 9th Tank Regiment launches the largest Japanese tank attack of the Pacific War. The Japanese tanks are annihilated by Marine weapons. A few days later, the surviving tanks fall victim to isolated M4A2s near Garapan.

July 24 to August 1   Battle for Tinian. The last day, three Ha-Gos are knocked out by Marine M4A2s.
July 21 to August 10   Battle for Guam. On six occasions the US Marine M4A2s come face to face with Type 95 Ha-Gos.
September 15 to November 27   Battle of Peleliu. On D-Day, the Tank Company, 14th Infantry Division's Ha-Gos attack the American beachhead. The assault is repulsed with the help of M4A2s from the 1st Tank Battalion.

The tank–infantry teams that appeared in the Marianas in the summer of 1944 proved to be very efficient in mop-up operations in the Central Pacific. Here on Saipan, a patrol is about to resume its progress. The column is led by a section of tanks from 1st Platoon, B Company, 2nd Tank Battalion. These tanks helped repulse the June 17 Japanese night attack. (NARA)

DESIGN AND DEVELOPMENT

THE TYPE 95 HA-GO

FAILED ATTEMPTS TO PRODUCE A HOMEMADE LIGHT TANK

When the tank appeared on the European battlefield in 1916, Japan, then an ally of the French and British, was immediately interested in the concept of the new weapon. It purchased its first tank from the British, about a month before the November 1918 Armistice. Other British and French models followed the next year, among them the Renault FT.

In the 1920s, European nations were reluctant to further export their more modern tanks to Japan. This led the Technical Bureau of the Imperial Japanese Army (IJA) to build its own tank. The IJA agreed to fund the project and after two years of development, the first Japanese-made tank appeared in 1927. This Japanese engineering debut was not satisfactory as the tank was too heavy: 18 tons.

The IJA was looking for a light tank (less than 10 tons) to be mass produced to support infantry in the field.

That same year, the British finally decided to sell the prototype of the Vickers light tank Type C to Japan. After acquiring it, Japan tested the vehicle. Unfortunately, the gasoline engine caught fire. This convinced the Japanese engineers to power future tanks with diesel-powered engines rather than gasoline.

Since the designers had successfully achieved construction of a first tank prototype, the IJA agreed to fund a second project. In the late 1920s, a new prototype was born.

A view of the cramped fighting compartment of a Type 95 from the driver's position looking back. It shows the bulkhead separating the crew from the engine compartment. Above the access door (center) is the air intake that injected room temperature to the engine by means of a pump located behind the door. Note the insulation panels on the walls and access door. While the rest of the crew compartment was insulated with asbestos panels, the engine compartment walls were insulated with pressed vegetable fiber, impregnated with ammonium dihydrogen phosphate to resist fire. Ammunition racks for the main gun and machine guns are visible to the right. (Author's collection)

Still too heavy—it weighed about 10 tons—the tank had satisfactory armor and was equipped with a 57mm main gun and a machine gun in a turret. The architecture of the turret would remain very specific to the Japanese tanks of pre-World War II development. While the main gun faced forward, the machine gun aimed backward. The tank commander could use either weapon, and aim the machine gun forward by rotating the turret. The prototype was approved and the production of the tank, designated Type 89, started in 1931.[1] Because of its weight, the vehicle was classified as a medium tank.

The vehicle was deployed to China and saw combat for the first time in February 1932 during the Shanghai Incident (a short but violent conflict in the city).

That same year a new prototype was approved as the Type 92. It was the first real light tank the Japanese produced as it weighed only 4 tons. It was fitted with two machine guns, one in a turret, the other in the hull. The light weight was obtained by sacrificing the tank's armor, which was reduced to ¼in. thick at the front. Such thin armor would barely protect the crew from machine-gun fire. Though not entirely satisfactory, the tank was developed and sent to Manchuria where it fought alongside the Type 89.

---

1   Tanks and other Japanese weapons were designated by the year the IJA approved them based on the Japanese calendar. For example, the Type 89 was approved in 2589 (1929 on the Gregorian calendar); the Type 95 in 2595 (1935).

This view of a destroyed Type 95 on Peleliu shows the typical design of Japanese World War II-era tank turrets, mounting two weapons opposite each other. The tank commander could use either the main gun or the machine gun. He would rotate the turret to aim the secondary weapon forward. (NARA)

TYPE 95 HA-GO,
9TH TANK REGIMENT

Shown here is an early production Type 95 Ha-Go from the 9th Regiment on Guam.

Early production Type 95 Ha-Go	
Length	4.38m
Width	2.06m
Height	2.15m
Main armament	37mm Type 94 main gun
Elevation	+20° to -15°
Number of rounds	121
Secondary armament	x 2 7.7mm Type 97 machine guns
Number of rounds	2,020 in 20-round clips
Engine	Mitsubishi NVD6 120, 6 cylinders, air cooled
Number of gears	4 forward and 1 reverse
Max speed on road	30mph

With the continuing conflict in China, the first two nationally designed tanks revealed their weaknesses. Owing to its weight, the Type 89 had difficulties keeping up with the infantry's advance when loaded aboard trucks, and the Type 92's firepower was not powerful enough to satisfactorily deal with Chinese resistance.

THE "THIRD CAR"

The Japanese infantry and cavalry schools decided to team up in the early 1930s to produce a new light tank prototype, following the IJA request to obtain a fast light tank equipped with a main gun. The designs of the two previous tanks both held some appeal, so engineers decided to combine them to produce the new tank.

The prototype, codenamed Ha-Go (the "Third Car," because it was the third tank designed by Japan), was achieved in 1934.[2] It retained the diesel engine of the Type 89B (diesel version of the Type 89), weighed 7.5 tons, and reached a maximum speed of 30mph. It mounted a 37mm main gun in the turret and a machine gun in the chassis.

It satisfactorily passed tests and, despite some criticism regarding its thin armor, a second prototype was built in 1935 with modifications drawn from previous trials. The astonishing maneuverability of the new light tank and its fit-for-purpose design led to its approval.

Before production started, several last-minute modifications were undertaken. The hull's design was widened at its center to increase the tank's ammunition storage capacities and the turret was modified to incorporate a machine gun aiming rearward, thus copying the Type 89's turret design.

Once combat loaded, the final vehicle's weight totaled 7.6 tons. Production began in 1936 under the designation of Type 95.

DESIGN

The Type 95 Ha-Go's armor was made of bolted armor plates, a common practice in the 1930s. It was crewed by three men: two in the hull and one in the turret. The only negotiable access to the crew compartment was the tank commander's hatch on the top of the turret. The driver's controls were located on the right-hand side of the hull; he sat on a square paddle, stuck between a bulky rack of 37mm rounds (at his back) and the final drive's box (on his left). The assistant driver sat on the floor, on the left-hand side of the tank's hull. He operated a ball-mounted 7.7mm machine gun and doubled as a mechanic, in charge of the engine.

The crew compartment was separated from the engine compartment by a wall. The engine remained accessible from inside, by means of a door. The inside of the crew compartment was insulated with woven asbestos padding, separated from the walls by an air pocket, to reduce radiation from the hull to the crew.

The turret was located on the left-hand side of the hull. The asymmetric location of turrets on Japanese tanks of the 1930s was another distinctive characteristic. It was a 360° rotating turret with no basket and no power traverse.

The tank commander, located behind the assistant driver, doubled as the gunner.

---

2   The term Ha-Go was not employed by Japanese tankmen. The tank was designated Type 95 by its users.

His position was very uncomfortable since only 65in. of headroom was available from the tank floor to the top hatch. He had to slouch to operate the turret weapons.

At the top of the turret was a split hatch, in which two little holes (with ports) allowed the commander to wave a flag from inside to communicate with surrounding vehicles. These ports also allowed fresh air to enter the vehicle and fumes to be ejected.

From inside, visibility was possible thanks to a series of vertical and horizontal slits cut in the tank's armor. Machine-gun fire concentrated on these slits often literally blinded the crew. To protect the driver's eyes, three bulletproof glass panels were installed directly behind the vision slits. When the tank was operating in a safe zone, the driver could open a large front hatch, which gave him better visibility.

The suspension system was composed of two double bogies on either side of the vehicle, supported through linkages by helical compression springs, protected by a curved 4mm armor plate. A curious modification of the suspension occurred after the vehicle was sent to Manchuria in the mid-1930s. The vehicle showed poor performance in the Manchurian fields compared to what was previously accepted. The vehicle's capacity was hampered by the local crops and the space between rows, which was the same as the space between each road wheel. The problem was solved by adding a small roller between the two road wheels of each bogie. The new design was known as the "Manchurian" suspension system as only the tanks fielded in Manchuria were equipped in this way.

The Type 95's hull and turret show a combined riveted and welded construction, typical of the 1930s. The hull panels were assembled around a channel and angle iron frame. This top view shows the holes in the split hatch used to wave flags from inside the tank to communicate with surrounding vehicles. (Author's collection)

PRODUCTION CHANGES

From 1936 to 1943, several changes occurred on the Ha-Go's production line, which led to minor modifications to the tank's external design. They were characterized by the addition of a reinforced steel ring around the tank commander's cupola; on later versions, rivets bolted to the hull and turret sides to stretch wires (to hang camouflage or equipment) were removed; the tow hook shape was improved and reinforced; and the front fenders' length was extended.

The most important modifications occurred inside the vehicle. Early Ha-Gos were equipped with two 6.5mm Type 91 machine guns, replaced by 7.7mm Type 97 machine guns in later models. From 1941, the Type 94 main gun was replaced by a Type 98 gun on the production line, allowing the tank commander to use antitank gun rounds (see *Technical Specifications*); the ammunition storage bins were maximized and re-designed; the electrical network was simplified; and the reserve fuel tank was re-designed.

Dates by which most of the changes were adopted on production lines seem not to have survived to the present day, but could have occurred at different times, varying

This front view of a restored Type 95 shows some of the particular features of the tank, such as the driver's hatch fully open to allow better visibility while driving, and the headlights turned to protect the bulbs from projectiles. To prevent raising dust while driving on dirt roads, each fender was fitted with two or three rubber leaves, as seen on the left-hand side of the photo. (Author's collection)

from one factory to another. Thus, it was common to find a mixture of older and newer features on the same vehicle and various combinations within the same unit.

COMBAT DEBUT

A handful of Type 95s saw combat for the first time in July 1937 in Quhar Province in China, where they acted in support of infantry. They proved valuable, as they were able to keep up with the infantry's advance, which faced little opposition.

The Ha-Go was more widely used during the Khalkhin Gol/Nomonhan Incident along the Mongolian border in June 1939 against the Soviets. The outcome of the battle was irrevocable: Japanese tanks, including the Type 95, were decidedly outmatched by Soviet tanks. The thin armor of the Japanese tanks was easily penetrated by 45mm main guns from Soviet tanks of the era, including the BT-7 light tank, the Ha-Go's counterpart. A Soviet study of a captured Ha-Go stated, in 1941, that the tank was—already—obsolete.

The Khalkhin Gol battle also showed that the Japanese 57mm gun that equipped the Type 97 Chi-Ha, a medium tank designed and produced in 1937 to replace the old Type 89, was not efficient at long ranges. This led the Japanese to produce a new turret equipped with a more powerful Type 01 47mm main gun. Old Type 97 turrets were replaced on newly produced vehicles; this freed a lot of 57mm-equipped turrets that the Japanese used to up-gun the Type 95s, giving birth to a handful of Type 4 Ke-Nu tanks by the end of the war.

Despite the disastrous results at Khalkhin Gol, the Ha-Go was produced until 1943 and fielded all around the Japanese Empire. It was still in use by many units at the time of the Japanese surrender in 1945. In all, 1,599 units of the Type 95 Ha-Go were produced, making it the most produced Japanese tank of the war.

POST-WAR CAREER

A total of 40 Type 95 tanks were sold to Thailand in 1940, which retained the Ha-Go in service until the 1950s. When France recovered its lost Indochina territories after the war,

French troops gather captured Japanese tanks, including Type 95s, to defend Phnom Penh, Indochina in October 1945. These vehicles show a series of field modifications, such as increased armor protection (which the crews were normally not allowed to carry out because of the scarcity of iron), the vertical bars made of iron, and the horizontal wooden plank to the rear of the tank for infantry to ride on. (The Tank Museum, Bovington)

large quantities of Japanese equipment were left behind, including several Type 95s. The French 5e Cuirassiers reused several Ha-Gos in combat in 1946 against the Viet-Minh.

THE M4A2 SHERMAN

MARINES UNDER ARMOR

When World War II broke out, the US Marines' experience with tanks was still very limited. Back in the 1920s, when the Marine Corps trained with the Navy as amphibious assault specialists, some Marine officers, veterans of the previous World War, urged the Corps to equip itself with tanks. As a matter of fact, naval gunfire and aircraft support was not accurate enough to provide the close support vital for infantry to deal with enemy beach defenses. On December 4, 1923, a three-tank platoon was hastily activated with old diesel-powered M1917 light tanks purchased from the Army. After nearly a decade of service and deployment in China in 1927, the Marine Corps decided it was time to modernize its armored fleet. Jointly with the US Navy, it funded the development of what is now considered a major misdirection in the Marine Corps tank procurement process: the turretless Marmon-Herrington CTL-3 tankette.

Born in 1935, its weight—5 tons—was limited by what ships' cranes and existing landing craft capacities could handle, and inevitably reduced the vehicle's protection and firepower. It was crewed by two men and armed with three .30-cal. machine guns. Moreover, the first variants of this tankette were mechanically weak and unreliable, but the civilian manufacturer kept improving the tank until 1941 with the Marine Corps' and Navy's consent.

Besides, the USMC held that the tank needed to be as light as possible to simplify the ship-to-shore approach under enemy fire. Conscious their tankette was not entirely satisfactory (the tankette's weaknesses were revealed during various trials), the Marine

Corps agreed to test Army-designed light tanks in 1940. The greater financial resources of the Army allowed more capacity for development and engineering than those of the Navy. Furthermore, Army tanks were known to be superior in terms of armor and firepower; they were then equipped with a 37mm main gun in a turret and several machine guns.

Though the Army light tanks (M2A2 and M2A4) proved satisfactory during the tests, the Marine Corps—perhaps through excess chauvinism—was reluctant to adopt them. But the situation in Europe in the summer of 1940 forced it to acquire the Army light tanks to quickly expand its armored force. Meanwhile, the Marmon Herrington tankettes were still developed, leading to improved turretless Marmon-Herrington CTL-6s and turreted Marmon-Herrington CTM-3TBDs.

In the meantime, the Navy and Marine Corps targeted the design and development of new types of landing craft, and called upon manufacturer Andrew J. Higgins. After several tries, in early 1941 Higgins proposed a 45ft Landing Craft Mechanized (LCM-2) equipped with a retractable bow ramp and capable of transporting a 20-ton light tank. The LCM-2 was followed by a larger model, the LCM-3, capable of transporting newly built Army 32-ton medium tanks.

The war in Europe followed by the entry of the United States into the war put a hasty end to the Marmon-Herrington tank adventure.

A few months after America declared war on Japan, Japanese forces started the construction of a new airfield in the Solomon Islands (South Pacific) that would threaten the approach to American territories and maritime routes to Australia. The Marines were then still training their newly born infantry divisions stateside for an expected deployment in the Pacific by early 1943.

The "national emergency" that resulted forced the Marine Corps to hastily acquire tanks in large numbers for its first two tank battalions, which would support its 1st and 2nd Marine divisions to be deployed in the Solomon Islands by August 1942. Army-designed light tanks were the only available solution.

THE ARMY MEDIUM TANK PROGRAM

Post-World War I, the US Army's armored force essentially relied on British- and French-designed tanks. In the 1920s, the Army decided it was time to design and manufacture its own tanks, including a medium-size type. Like in World War I, the purpose of the tank was to break and exploit breaches in enemy defensive lines in direct support of infantry.

During the 1920s to 1930s, several attempts were made to build a newly designed medium tank, but they proved unsatisfactory owing to either mechanical weaknesses or underpowered engines.

In the late 1930s, medium tanks mounting a 37mm main gun in a turret were being developed, but the war in Europe showed that main guns under 75mm and lightly armored medium tanks were totally obsolete. Nonetheless, the technology to set up a 75mm gun in a tank turret was not yet available to the US. In 1940, a temporary solution was found with the M3 medium tank, mounting a 75mm gun in the chassis and a 37mm in a turret.

Meanwhile, the search for a tank mounting a 75mm gun in a rotating turret began. It had to use as many parts from the M3 as possible to reduce the time dedicated to production-line model conversion.

In 1941, the T-6 prototype designed by the Ordnance showed up. It mounted a 75mm main gun and a co-axial .30-cal. machine gun in a turret, retained the same suspension system as the M3, and had thicker armor. It weighed about 30 tons. After several technical improvements, it was approved by the Armored Forces. Its production was standardized and began in February 1942. The new tank was designated medium tank M4.

Several variants of the M4 were built and were differentiated by their engines. There was not time enough to design a specific engine for the vehicle, and medium tanks were equipped either with multiple car and truck engines or even aircraft engines to deliver enough power (see Table 1). The diesel version, the M4A2, produced from

Only a handful of M4A4s reached the Marine Corps training centers in California. As it turned out, the five Chrysler car engines that powered the tank were highly unpopular because of difficulties in maintaining and synchronizing them. This Marine Corps M4A4 shows an unusual configuration as it has been modified to carry fully equipped Marines around the battlefield. (MCHD)

The M4A2 was the first version the Marines could get in large numbers from the Army and in a minimum of time. After Tarawa, the Marines equipped their tanks with wading stacks to cross the island's reefs. On Saipan, many M4A2s from the 2nd Tank Battalion were not correctly waterproofed and stalled on their way to the shore, despite the wading stacks. (NARA)

April 1942, was the one the Marine Corps would use the most during World War II.

The M4A2 tank was a high-silhouetted vehicle with a welded hull, with vertical sides (called sponsons) and a 56° front glacis (called the slope) from the vertical with two protruding hoods. On the top of each one was an access hatch to the hull's crew compartment. The driver sat to the left; the assistant driver, who also operated a bow machine gun, sat to the right. The hatches were so narrow that a crew member equipped with a pistol belt could easily be hindered while exiting. This problem was solved with a second design featuring larger hatches. The slope was then made of a single piece, with an angle of 47° from the vertical, which greatly improved the ballistic performance of the front armor. Beneath the tank, behind the assistant driver's seat, was an emergency hatch that allowed the crew to exit under the cover of the tank's hull.

The rear of the tank was the most vulnerable part. It contained the engines with air intakes on the top and access doors at the stern. The experience gained at Tarawa led the Marine Corps to equip the tanks with two exhausts, one on the engine deck, the other to the rear. This prevented water from entering the engine compartment once it was properly sealed with greased tapes. Once ashore, the exhausts were disassembled by the crew.

The turret was located on the top center of the hull and was fitted with a basket. It was a 360° rotating turret and contained three crew members: the gunner, loader, and tank commander. On early models, the commander's hatch was the only access for the three men, and in an emergency evacuation, one of the three—usually the loader—remained trapped inside the tank.

M4A2, TANK COMPANY, 4TH MARINES

Shown here is a mid-production M4A2 Sherman. Its unit symbol is a charging rhino.

Mid-production M4A2 Sherman	
Length	5.91m
Width	2.62m
Height	2.74m
Main armament	75mm M3 gun
Elevation	+25° to -10°
Number of rounds	140 (modified)
Secondary armament	x 3 .30-cal. machine guns
Number of rounds	14,000 in 250-round belts (modified)
Engine	Twin General Motors 6046, 12 cylinders, water cooled
Number of gears	5 forward and 1 reverse
Max speed on road	30mph

Late turret models included a second hatch for the loader's use. Once entirely buttoned up, visibility from inside was made possible thanks to rotating periscopes. The gunner had a specific fixed periscope, synchronized with the main armament.

Table 1: Sherman variants' motorization

Main variants	Engines	Origin
M4 and M4A1	Continental R975	Aircraft
M4A2	General Motors 6046	Truck
M4A3	Ford GAA V8	Aircraft (reconditioned)
M4A4	Chrysler A57 multibank	Car

All variants used the same spare parts except, obviously, engine parts. This greatly simplified the production and assembly lines. This permitted a quick response to the need to produce reliable equipment in a minimum of time and at low cost. In all, America produced nearly 50,000 Shermans during the war, of which 8,053 were M4A2s armed with a 75mm main gun.

THE MEDIUM TANKS IN MARINE CORPS USE

The Marine Corps was immediately interested in the Sherman's firepower, far superior to the light tanks then in use by the divisional tank battalions (M2A4s and M3 variants).[3]

The Marine Corps' intention was to form two independent medium tank battalions (only one was actually activated) from which individual tank companies would be loaned to infantry divisions to be used in support of light tanks during operations.

The first medium tanks the Marine Corps obtained from the Army were the M4A4 variant. Initially, 22 vehicles were shipped to the Corps by late 1942, so that tank crews and mechanics could familiarize themselves with the new weapon. But the complexity of its engine made it unpopular.

The US Army retained all M4s and M4A1s, but the M4A3s were not produced in sufficient number at that time to equip the USMC.[4] The M4A4 variant was accepted by the British, Commonwealth and Free French Forces, who considered it combat worthy.

The M4A2 was shipped to the above foreign nations as well as to the Soviets, whose shipments took priority. However, production was sufficient to equip the Marine Corps, since the US Army was reluctant to use the A2 variant, quoting reliability and maintenance problems.

Thus, the diesel version of the M4 was the first one the Corps could quickly obtain in large numbers.

---

3   Marines never used the name "Sherman." They used the term "medium tank" to designate the M4. However, the name "Sherman"—given by the British—was frequently used by American war correspondents and thus commonly encountered in newspapers and magazines during World War II.

4   24 M4A1s were, however, made available to A Company 1st Tank Battalion while in Australia in 1943, the only ones the Marines ever operated.

The USMC obtained its first M4A2s by early 1943. They equipped the 1st Corps Tank Battalion (medium), from which one company was used for the first time at Tarawa in November of the same year. The experience gained during the battle proved the Marine Corps needed to convert its divisional tank battalions to all medium-tank battalions. Indeed, the 37mm main gun of the light tanks proved incapable of reducing Japanese fortifications during the battle.

In 1944, the Marine Corps tank battalions were progressively converted to the M4A2; the light tanks were relayed to secondary roles, and were definitively abandoned after the Marianas operation.

By late 1944 to early 1945, the Marine Corps decided to convert to the M4A3 (gasoline engine) variant, now available in large quantities, for fear of the M4A2 production lines shutting before the end of the war.[5] Criticism came from the tank crews, who liked the reliability of the A2 version and the safety of the diesel fuel, which rarely caught fire even when the engines were damaged.

By the end of the war, of the six tank battalions the Marine Corps had, three retained the M4A2 (1st, 2nd, and 3rd Tank battalions) and the other three had converted to the M4A3 (4th, 5th, and 6th Tank battalions).

The combat career of the M4A2 within the Marine Corps lasted until the 1st Tank Battalion departed Tientsin in China in 1947, leaving its battered vehicles behind.

On Peleliu, the crew of the M4A2 B13 Liz take a break after sawing the damaged barrel of the main gun. Note the large hatches on this late-production model. (NARA)

---

5 The M4A2 was produced until May 1945.

TECHNICAL SPECIFICATIONS

ARMAMENT

The M4A2 was equipped with an M3 75mm main gun and two 7.62mm M1919A4 machine guns, one mounted in the hull, the other mounted parallel to the main gun. A third machine gun could be mounted on the turret top, but was seldom used. In the close combat of the Pacific, tank crews generally operated buttoned up. In the absence of any standardization, the model of machine gun varied from one tank company to another. Some preferred to operate a 12.7mm M2 anti-aircraft machine gun, but the most commonly used was an additional M1919A4. On Guam, the hull-mounted machine gun was replaced by an E4-5 flame-thrower in six M4A2s from the 3rd Tank Battalion. The replaced machine gun was carried inside the tank. The E4-5 was a small-capacity flame-thrower, and once all the fuel was expended, the bow gunner could switch from the flame gun to the machine gun. Although unsatisfactory, these flame-throwers were used until the end of the war by the Marine Corps tank battalions.

The Ha-Go main weapon was a 37mm gun (Type 94 or 98) mounted in the turret. When the turret was stationary, the main gun had a free traverse of 10° to the right and to the left. Two 7.7mm Type 97 machine guns were mounted in the tank: one in the hull pointing forward, the other pointing backward mounted on the rear right of the turret.[6] Both the turret machine gun and main gun were manned by the tank commander.

---

6   Early versions of the Type 95 were equipped with a 6.5mm Type 91 machine gun.

M4A2 MAIN GUN SIGHT

TYPE 95 MAIN GUN SIGHT

US .30-CAL. MACHINE-GUN PERISCOPE

JAPANESE 7.7MM TYPE 97 MACHINE-GUN SIGHT

GUNNERY

In the Sherman, the turret traverse mechanism was primarily hydraulic, which allowed the gunner to accurately and quickly aim at the target. If damaged, the system could be disengaged, and the gunner could rotate the turret manually. Moreover, a gyrostabilizer allowed him to aim at his target while the tank was moving.

The American gunner had a choice of two sights. The first and most used was a periscope (M3 or M4 model) with a telescope enclosed inside. Several versions of telescopes were used. Some had no magnification (model M32) while others had a 1.5-power magnification (models M38 and M40).

The M32's reticle was graduated in yards with its center adjusted on 600yd. The first graduation (dot) below its center indicated 1,000yd, then range dots and lines were at 500yd intervals. Horizontal lines (deflection lines) represented 10 mils. The center circle's radius indicated 5 mils. A mil represents one yard at 1,000yd distance. The device was used against moving targets.

The second choice available to the Marine tank gunner was a direct sight telescope M55 with a 3-power magnification (replaced by the M70 telescope by 1944).

Owing to the short ranges imposed by the topography of the Central Pacific islands, most Marine gunners used only the periscope. In some cases, the direct sight telescope was replaced by an additional M1919A4 machine gun, or simply removed and the hole through the gunshield was sealed. In the hull, the bow gunner used his unmarked periscope to see where his bullets hit and used his tracers (one tracer every five bullets) to walk the fire onto the target.

In the Ha-Go, the tank gunner (and commander) had to manually traverse the turret and aim at the enemy with a shoulder harness, similar to that used in World War I-era tanks.

The Japanese tank gunner had no choice but to use the telescope attached to the 37mm main gun. It was a 2-power magnification direct sight periscope manufactured by Nikko. It allowed 20° visibility outside. Its reticle markings were at 200m intervals, up to 2,000m. Two lenses, one red, the other yellow, were available to the gunner to modify the sight's brightness and contrast.

In the Type 95, the turret and hull's Type 97 machine guns had their own telescope. It was a 1.5-power direct sight telescope with a 30° angle of view. The center of the cross-hair was calibrated on 100m, then graduations succeeded as follows: 500m, 700m, 900m, 1,000m, 1,200m, 1,400m. On the reticle, three ellipses corresponding to the weapon's cone of dispersion were marked. Below 1,600m a bullet would strike within the first ellipse; between 1,600 and 3,200m a bullet would strike within the second ellipse; and between 3,200 and 4,800m a bullet would strike within the third ellipse. This was particularly useful for indirect fire purposes.

MAIN GUN AMMUNITION

1. M48 HE round (75mm)—M3 gun
2. M72 AP round (75mm)—M3 gun
3. T30 Canister round (75mm)—M3 gun
4. Type 94 AP round (37mm)—Type 94 gun
5. Type 94 HE round (37mm)—Type 94 gun
6. Type 94 HE round (37mm)—Type 98 gun
7. Type 94 AP round (37mm)—Type 98 gun

	Comparison of round sizes						
	Japanese				**US**		
Type of round	Type 94 HE (Type 94 gun)	Type 94 AP (Type 94 gun)	Type 94 HE (Type 98 gun)	Type 94 AP (Type 98 gun)	M72 AP (M3 gun)	M48 HE (M3 gun)	T30 Canister (M3 gun)
Length (fused)	10.1in.	8.97in.	11.34in.	10.2in.	20.81in.	26.6in.	26.0in.
Case length	5.3in.	5.3in.	6.5in.	6.5in.	13.82in.	13.82in.	13.82in.

MAIN GUN AMMUNITION

A wide variety of ammunition was available for the M3 main gun of the Sherman tank. The composition and number of shells evolved with the conflict. Lacking prior experience, the tankers of C Company, 1st Corps Tank Battalion (medium) brought in the allotted number of 75mm rounds per tank, i.e. 97 rounds. Three types of round were then used: the high-explosive (HE) M48, the armor-piercing (AP) M72, and the canister T30 round. The ammunition supply being unpredictable on Tarawa, the tank crews would use the pack-howitzer 75mm round as a last resort.

With experience, the number of rounds was increased by welding extra ammunition racks on the turret's deck and walls. Prior to Peleliu, the 1st Tank Battalion increased the total number of rounds per tank from 97 to 117. A Company, 2nd Tank Battalion increased the number of rounds to 125 prior to Saipan.

The M48 HE round with either the M48 or M54 fuse was the most extensively used projectile. Crews would set up the fuse either on "super-quick" (to explode at the moment of contact with a rough surface, such as a steel plate) or "delay" (for use against open-top emplacements, such as trenches; by firing it at the ground, the shell ricocheted and exploded above the open-top emplacement, killing the occupants).

After Tarawa, the M61 armor-piercing capped ammunition (APC) replaced the M72 AP round and the white phosphorous (WP) round or smoke M64 came in addition.

The HE round was the most effective against Japanese fortifications and tanks. Tankers complained about the AP and APC rounds' power. Against armor, it went straight through. The APHE (Armor Piercing High-Explosive) was seldom used.

As was often the case in the Marine Corps of that era, there was no standardization. Each unit, even within the same battalion, made its own decision regarding the unit of fire's composition.

The Japanese gunner in the Ha-Go had a more restricted choice. Two types of round were available: the Type 94 HE round and the Type 94 AP round. The latter was intended to be substituted by the Type 1 AP round, but it never materialized.

The Type 98 main gun that equipped the late models of Ha-Go used the same projectiles as the Type 94 antitank gun. The Type 94 antitank gun and the Ha-Go's Type 94 main gun were of identical caliber (37mm) and bore the same number, but were designed for different purposes. The Type 94 tank gun had a shorter chamber than that of the antitank gun. Thus, the cartridge size was shorter in the case of the tank ammunition (5.27in.) than that of the antitank gun (6.54in.). The chamber of the Type 98 tank gun being longer, it allowed the employment of the antitank gun ammunition, which contained more propellant.

The tank carried a total of 121 rounds of 37mm when equipped with the Type 94 gun, and 122 rounds when mounting the Type 98 main gun.

Type of round	Type 94 HE (Type 94 gun)	Type 94 AP (Type 94 gun)	Type 94 HE (Type 98 gun)	Type 94 AP (Type 98 gun)	M61 APC (M3 gun)	M72 AP (M3 gun)	M48 HE (M3 gun)
Weight (fused)	2.15lb	2.27lb	2.54lb	2.67lb	19.92lb	18.80lb	18.80lb
Length (fused)	10.1in.	8.97in.	11.34in.	10.2in.	26.29in.	20.81in.	26.6in.
Muzzle velocity	1,900 f/s	1,880 f/s	Unknown 2,320 f/s when fired from Type 94 antitank gun	Unknown 2,300 f/s when fired from Type 94 antitank gun	1,930 f/s	1,930 f/s	1,470 f/s
Armor penetration 1,000yd (homogeneous steel, 30° obliquity)		0.83in.		Unknown 2in. at 100yd	2.4in.	2.5in.	
Weight (fused)	2.15lb	2.27lb	2.54lb	2.67lb	19.92lb	18.80lb	18.80lb

Table 2: Main gun ammunition comparison

ARMOR

Both vehicles had somewhat different armor thickness. Table 3 shows how thin the Type 95 armor was, demonstrating its vulnerability to almost every weapon above the

The company commander's tank of the Tank Company, 22nd Marines on Guam sports wooden planks to increase its side protection against Japanese antitank weapons. However, the Type 01 47mm antitank gun AP ammunition was able to penetrate the tank's hull despite the increased armor. This led the Marines to fill in the airspace between the hull and planks with concrete, or to use steel plating instead of wood in future operations. (NARA)

.30-cal. the Marines had. The M4A2 armor was not particularly thick, but satisfactory for the Pacific Theater, though some Japanese antitank weapons were capable of penetrating its sides. This led to some field modifications, such as the addition of wooden boards, bolted on U-shaped bars welded on the tank's sides to prevent rounds from penetrating the sponsons.

The M4A2 proved vulnerable (on its rear and sides) to the Type 94 antitank gun at very close ranges (<200yd) during the Tarawa operation. However, the gun-tank version was not powerful enough to damage the Sherman's armor. The barrel was too short and the ammunition case contained too little propellant to give the round enough speed to penetrate a Sherman's hull or turret.

Table 3: Armor thickness compared		
	Type 95 Ha-Go	M4A2
Turret front	0.47in.	3.0in.
Turret sides	0.47in.	2.0in.
Turret rear	0.47in.	2.0in.
Hull front	0.47in.	2.0in. (mid production) 2.5in. (late production)
Hull sides	0.47in. front; 0.39in. rear	1.5in.
Hull rear	0.47in.	1.5in.

COMMUNICATIONS

To communicate, Marines installed US Navy amplitude modulated radios available in large numbers. They were composed of a transmitter (GF) and a receiver (RU), provided with about 50 coils that allowed the radio operator to change frequencies.

The "Ruji-fuji" allowed the tank crew members to communicate with each other via an internal communication system. In practice, the roaring of the twin diesel engine and noise of gunfire rendered understanding extremely difficult, but it worked. This radio also allowed communication with other surrounding vehicles fitted with the same GF/RU radio, plugged in to the same frequency.

These GF/RUs were designed in the 1930s for aircraft, not for use in a hot and humid, confined space like a tank turret. At Eniwetok, serious interference from aircraft traffic hampered communications. These problems and the complexity of the radio's use caused the tank crews to seldom use the GF/RU at Tarawa.

Despite reliability problems, this radio was still used in Marine tanks during the Marianas campaign in mid-1944. For the assault on Peleliu in September 1944, the 1st Tank Battalion switched to more reliable frequency-modulated radios: the SCR-508 and SCR-528.

The Japanese had more rudimentary communication systems. In theory, only the leaders from regiment down to platoon levels had tanks fitted with a radio. When the command tank was a Ha-Go, it was equipped either with a Type 306 or Type 96 Mark 4E radio set. Both sets were short-range radios: approximately 2½- to 3¾-mile theoretical range when the tank was stationary. The range was halved when in motion. Radio-equipped vehicles were easily recognizable thanks to a rail-shaped antenna on the turret.

In practice, most communications were by hand or flag signals, or by runners, leaving space for misunderstanding. A platoon leader would systematically use the physical communication way to "talk down" to the tanks under him.

Tank companies entirely equipped with Type 95 Ha-Gos did not always include radio-installed vehicles. By 1944, regimental tank commanders operated from more modern vehicles such as the Type 97 medium tank, equipped with more reliable radios. Tank units were then composed of a mixture of two or three tank models (see *The Combatants*).

In 1935, tanks from most nations lacked intercom systems. Tank commanders, who usually stood behind the driver, gave instructions by kicking him in the shoulders or the head: a very unpleasant situation for the driver. Within the Ha-Go, the configuration prevented any physical communication between the tank commander and the driver: the former was located behind the assistant driver (see *Design and Development*). Instead, the Japanese designed a rudimentary system of voice pipe and earphones for the tank commander to communicate orders down to the driver. It was

Marines from the 4th Division undergoing training in May 1945. The squad leader is using the tank–infantry telephone to provide information on enemy positions, invisible from inside the tank. Even with a 50ft cord that allowed the user to adopt a prone position, the use of the telephone remained dangerous for infantry. (NARA)

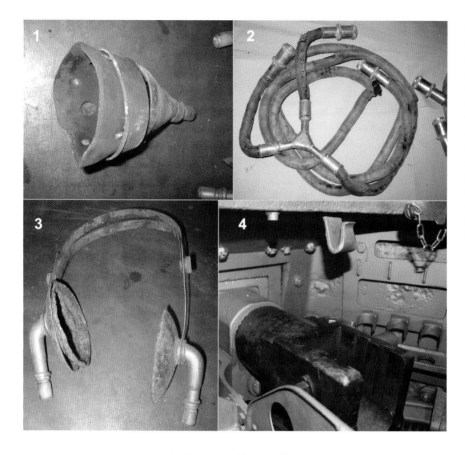

The intercom system of the Ha-Go was composed of a three-part set that was entirely removable. The mouthpiece (1) was plugged into a pipe (2) fitted with a Y-shaped distributor that relayed the message via two sub-pipes, connected to the driver's headphones (3). The set was to remain close at hand when the tank was in motion. Hence, the tank commander could hang the speaking device on a small hook (4) located above the main gun's breech. (Oliver Barnham)

a one-way intercom system: the driver could not talk back to the commander. It was composed of a mouthpiece (used by the commander) plugged into a pipe connected to earpieces worn over the driver's head. The three-part set was entirely removable and stored in a box to the left-hand side of the driver.

FIELD TELEPHONE—FAKE RIVET

Both vehicles were originally designed for an infantry support role. The Type 95 showed up with a button on its rear armor plate for "communication" purposes. This button was activated by infantry to inform the tank crews of their presence around the vehicle. The button appeared to be a rivet and was dissimulated among other "real" ones. It activated a horn, located above the transmission bloc. Though it was not for direct communication, this system was ahead of its time in 1935.

When the M4A2 appeared in the Pacific Theater, it was not equipped to communicate with the environment outside. Its radio was incompatible with the infantry portable radios. Rudimentary methods were then used to communicate: a reconnaissance guide walking in front of the tank would point his rifle in the general direction of the target and indicated the distance by hand signal. When trained guides were not available, the infantry would crawl on the turret to talk to the tank

The red arrow indicates the position of the "fake rivet" on the Type 95, which allowed infantry to warn the tank crew of their presence around the vehicle. The rivet activated a horn (see bottom-right inset), located above the transmission cover, to the front left of the driver. (Author's collection)

The Marines liked the twin diesel engine of the M4A2 because of its reliability and easy maintenance. Moreover, the tank could be maneuvered with a single engine if one of the two was knocked out. This tank, from the 1st Tank Battalion, is undergoing thorough inspection on Banika, Russell Islands, 1944. (NARA)

commander, or the tank commander descended from the vehicle. In either case, many casualties were caused by these methods during the war.

On Eniwetok, the 2nd Separate Tank Company fitted microphones on the rear of its tanks for infantry to use. A system of green and red flags was also tried for stop or go signals, but it was unsatisfactory and was abandoned.

From experience gained at Tarawa and in the Marshall Islands, the Marines installed French-style phones (transmitter and receiver) on the rear of their tanks. The first large-scale use of telephones for tank–infantry communication occurred during the Marianas campaign. Despite the fact that phones often fell victim to enemy fire or technical deficiencies, the system was standardized throughout each tank battalion.

MOBILITY AND POWER

Both vehicles differed in size, weight, and power. In almost all criteria, the Ha-Go was outmatched by the Sherman. The only advantage the Ha-Go had over its larger opponent was its speed and mobility off road—even on soft ground, thanks to its low ground pressure.

Table 4: Technical capacities compared		
	Type 95 Ha-Go	M4A2
Combat weight (without field modifications)	7.6 tons	32 tons
Engine	6 cylinders, air-cooled diesel engine, Mitsubishi NVD6 120	6 cylinders per water-cooled diesel engine (twin), General Motors 6046
Horsepower	110hp	375hp
Power-to-weight ratio	14.5hp/ton	11.7hp/ton
Road speed	30mph	30mph
Fuel tank capacity	29gal	148gal
Range	110 miles	150 miles
Ground pressure	8.7psi	13.2psi
Maximum slope the tank can negotiate (ascending and descending)	45 percent	60 percent

ASSESSMENT

The M4A2 and Type 95 tanks were very different from one another. The Type 95 Ha-Go was a good tank for its era (i.e. the mid-1930s) and perfectly fulfilled the role of supporting the infantry that it was designed for. It matched its American counterparts of the time, the M2 and M3 light tanks, which were of similar design and technical capacity.

However, the Type 95 was emphatically outclassed by the medium tank M4A2. As described above, the Sherman was a product of American technology of the early 1940s and was technically far superior to the Ha-Go. On paper, the Ha-Go had no chance of survival if opposed by the Sherman. But the Japanese combatants' tenacity and fighting spirit added another dimension to the tank duels that took place.

THE STRATEGIC SITUATION

Following Germany's defeat in World War I, Japan—then an ally of the French, British, and US—was given authority over the former German territories in the Pacific. Hence, the Mariana (apart from Guam), Caroline, and Marshall islands were mandated to the Japanese Empire by the League of Nations.

Meanwhile, Japan was beginning a rapid and large-scale modernization of its industry, which would mobilize more resources than it could itself produce. Neighboring East and Southeast Asian countries concentrated a myriad of resources such as rubber, oil, and ore, which Japan would soon need if it wanted to pursue modernization. The situation was an obvious threat to the Americans, whose possessions in the Pacific would be greatly weakened by Japanese expansion.

In the 1920s, the United States anticipated future wars against foreign nations. To face each conflict, the US established color-coded plans to deal with each nation. "War Plan Orange" foresaw a conflict in the Pacific against Japan in which the US Navy would have to defeat the Imperial Japanese Navy near Japan's Home Islands.

In 1921, Marine Corps Major Earl H. Ellis and his staff established the basics of an amphibious doctrine. Because of the Japanese mandated islands and the need to resupply the fleet in transit, it would be necessary to take islands from the enemy to establish advance bases. Somehow, Ellis and his staff anticipated a Central Pacific war nearly two decades before it materialized.

From then on, the Marine Corps was destined to wage an island war and capture advance bases for the Navy to anchor and resupply.

Triangle 1 Butcher, the command tank of Captain Bertram A. Yaffe, of B Company, 3rd Tank Battalion on Guam. Note that the straight telescope has been removed and the hole through the gunshield sealed. This tank was involved in a race against a Japanese Type 95 Ha-Go through American lines on August 2, 1944. (MCHD)

While the US Marine Corps and Navy began training and testing its new amphibious doctrine, Japan's expansionism materialized in 1931 with the annexation of Manchuria. This province would soon become the hometown of the Kwantung Army and the primary training site for Imperial Japanese Army tank men. On July 7, 1937, Japanese and Chinese forces confronted each other in the Marco Polo Bridge Incident, igniting the Second Sino-Japanese War. The Japanese, better organized and equipped, overwhelmed the Chinese defenders and eventually conquered key towns on the southeastern Chinese shore, thus cutting Chinese resupply maritime routes.

In 1939, Japanese and Soviet forces fought each other in a series of battles along the Manchurian/Mongol border. The Khalkhin Gol/Nomonhan Incident of May 1939 led to a disastrous Japanese tactical defeat in September that year. The defeat made them realize that their hopes of gaining territories in Siberia were now futile. Among other points, this defeat also highlighted the obsolescence of Japanese tanks and the urgent need to modernize and increase the tank fleet.

But Japan's war effort was prioritizing aircraft and battleship development. A small-scale development was, however, undertaken to up-gun existing tank designs. In the 1940s, newly designed turret tanks appeared, among them the improved Type 97 Shinhoto Chi-Ha, mounting the powerful Type 01 47mm antitank gun.[7] (See Osprey Duel 43: *M4 Sherman vs Type 97 Chi-Ha* by Steven Zaloga.)

To the south, territories were under the control of Western powers. Japan, despite its ambitions, was not ready to fight against European colonies. But things changed in the summer of 1940, when the Dutch and French were defeated by Nazi Germany and Great Britain prepared to be invaded. Japan resumed its expansion to the south with the occupation of some key airfields in northern French Indochina. This situation

7   As with the term "Ha-Go," the term Shinhoto Chi-Ha was not used by the men in the field. The tank
    was known as the Type 97 with the 47mm gun.

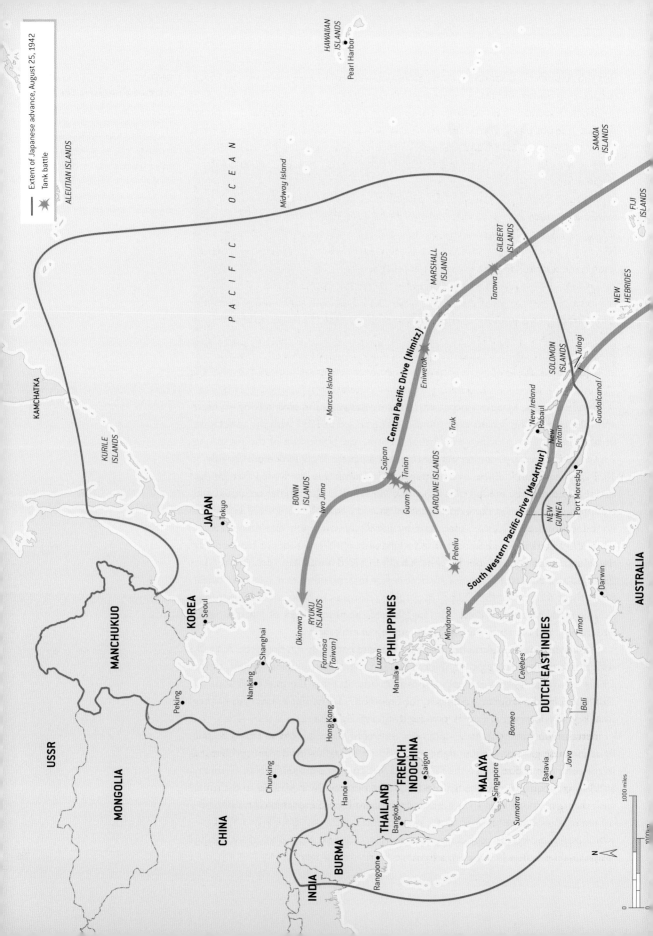

ALEUTIAN ISLANDS

HAWAIIAN ISLANDS
Pearl Harbor

PACIFIC OCEAN

Midway Island

SAMOA ISLANDS

FIJI ISLANDS

KAMCHATKA

Marcus Island

MARSHALL ISLANDS

Tarawa

GILBERT ISLANDS

NEW HEBRIDES

KURILE ISLANDS

Central Pacific Drive (Nimitz)

Eniwetok

Truk

CAROLINE ISLANDS

New Ireland

Rabaul

New Britain

SOLOMON ISLANDS

Tulagi

Guadalcanal

USSR

MONGOLIA

MANCHUKUO

JAPAN
Tokyo

KOREA
Seoul

Peking

Nanking

Shanghai

BONIN ISLANDS

Iwo Jima

Saipan
Tinian
Guam

Peleliu

South Western Pacific Drive (MacArthur)

Port Moresby

NEW GUINEA

CHINA

Chunking

Hong Kong

Okinawa

RYUKU ISLANDS

Formosa [Taiwan]

Luzon

PHILIPPINES

Manila

Mindanao

Celebes

Timor

Darwin

AUSTRALIA

Hanoi

THAILAND

Bangkok

FRENCH INDOCHINA

Saigon

MALAYA

Singapore

Sumatra

Batavia

Borneo

Java

Bali

DUTCH EAST INDIES

BURMA

Rangoon

INDIA

N

1000 miles

1000 km

0

led the Americans to set up an embargo on kerosene and iron exportation to Japan, with only a limited impact.

Japan desperately needed the natural resources from Malaya and the Dutch East Indies. A major problem was that the Dutch Government fled to Great Britain when Nazi Germany attacked and was now, together with its colonies, under British protection. To make things worse, Great Britain was an important ally of the United Sates.

Though Japan felt unprepared for a conflict with the United States, the situation made a conflict against occidental powers in Asia and in the Pacific inevitable. Moreover, the April 1941 Soviet–Japanese Neutrality Pact and the long struggle the German Army faced against the Red Army in the plains of western Russia definitively closed the door to Japanese expansion in Siberia.

In July 1941, the Vichy French Government, under pressure from the Japanese Empire, allowed the Japanese to occupy southern Indochina, including its airfields and harbors. This unpleasant situation led the Americans to set up an embargo on oil exportation, which actually turned out to be a total embargo on commercial exchanges with Japan. Though American-Japanese negotiations attempted to find a solution to the embargo—Japan desperately needed American oil and the Americans knew that this embargo would accelerate the Japanese drive on the Dutch East Indies—they achieved no positive results. By December 1, 1941, Japan decided that a conflict with the United States was inevitable and would soon materialize.

On December 7–8, Japanese forces launched a series of simultaneous assaults on various British- and US-held territories in Asia and in the Pacific. Japanese air and naval forces attacked the American base at Pearl Harbor, Hawaii that same day in an attempt to prevent a quick American intervention in the Pacific.

But Japan's attack on Pearl Harbor only partially disabled the American fleet in the Pacific: carriers were absent when the Japanese attacked, and most fuel depots remained untouched. Worse, it accelerated the United States' entry into World War II, on December 8, 1941.

By late 1941 to early 1942, the Japanese succeeded in capturing Guam (December 10), the Gilbert Islands (December 10), Wake (December 23), the Dutch East Indies (March 9), and the Philippines (May 8) among many others.

The Japanese onslaught in the Pacific culminated in the summer of 1942. The US Navy inflicted its first defeat on the Imperial Japanese Navy at the Battle of Midway in June. Japan's blitzkrieg in the Pacific came to a halt for the first time. In August, US Forces operated a series of landings in the Solomons. The island of Guadalcanal held the key to victory, because it possessed an airfield. Simultaneously, a raid was undertaken on Butaritari, an island in the Gilbert Islands chain, to create a diversion. The Japanese garrison on the island was annihilated and facilities damaged, leading the Japanese to realize the vulnerability of their outlying territories.

As a consequence, Japan began fortifying islands, and built airfields and facilities on the larger ones. The island of Betio (Tarawa Atoll), in the Gilbert Islands, was one of many islands to be fortified in this way. The statement of Admiral Keiji Shibazaki, who commanded the garrison, illustrates Japan's will to render these islands impregnable: "a hundred men in a hundred years couldn't take Tarawa."

This captured Type 95 Ha-Go is undergoing inspection by members of the 3rd Tank Battalion on Guam. Captured tanks were often a matter of curiosity to American tankers. The white band and kanji character on the turret indicate a vehicle of the divisional Tank Unit, 29th Division. (NARA)

At the time, Japan's water's edge defense doctrine was not intended to prevent an enemy landing, but to earn time. The *Yogaki* or waylaying attack was based on active defense before resuming the offensive. Slowing down the enemy assault on the beach would immobilize the US Fleet ashore long enough for the Imperial Japanese Navy to reach the battlefield from the formidable base of Truk in the Marshall Islands and annihilate the static American vessels.

On the ground, Japanese water's edge defense doctrine often materialized as a series of more or less coordinated tank–infantry counterattacks. Commonly known as the "banzai" charges to the Americans, they frequently resulted in the annihilation of the Japanese counterattack force, outclassed by American firepower.

The American strategy in the Pacific would follow two routes: a drive through the Central Pacific (Admiral Chester Nimitz) and a Southwest Pacific drive (General Douglas MacArthur). Both drives would carefully isolate the centers of resistance of Rabaul and Truk, and converge on Formosa.

The Central Pacific drive would bring the Japanese Type 95 Ha-Go and the US Marine Corps M4A2 Sherman face to face in brutally unbalanced confrontations at Tarawa, Eniwetok (Marshall Islands), in the Marianas, and on Peleliu.

TARAWA AND THE MARSHALL ISLANDS

The Central Pacific drive began in November 1943 at Tarawa, where the Japanese had built an airfield on Betio that would be vital to help take the Marshall Islands, supposed to be more heavily defended. US bombers based on Betio would neutralize strategic objectives and help seize areas around the next objectives.

Tarawa would be a "first" in many aspects for the Americans. At Guadalcanal, the landings faced almost no opposition because the Japanese had fled into the jungle.

This time, an assault conducted against heavily defended beaches was to be undertaken for the first time in the war. Somehow, Tarawa would serve as a large-scale rehearsal, in real conditions, to test the doctrine of amphibious assaults for future operations in the Central Pacific.

Tarawa was also the first time the US Marine Corps utilized the medium tank Sherman in combat. At first, it was supposed to land after the light tanks to exploit breaches in Japanese beach defenses. But hydrographic conditions, fierce opposition, and logistical issues forced the Marines to land the medium tanks in direct support of infantry on D-Day. Tarawa would also see the first Sherman versus Ha-Go duel of the war.

The 72-hour struggle on Betio greatly improved the "defended beach assault" doctrine. Among many other aspects, tank–infantry coordination and communications were greatly emphasized during training and improved upon; tanks were equipped with fording equipment preventing their loss while crossing reefs; and medium tanks progressively replaced light tanks within tank battalions—their firepower and armor being better suited to dealing with Japanese defenses.

Following the capture of Tarawa, the front line moved into the Marshall Islands. Contrary to what was expected, the islands in this chain were not as heavily fortified as Betio. The rapidity with which they were captured (and Truk isolated) surprised both sides. At the time of their loss, Japanese doctrine was beginning to evolve. But the Americans were determined to exploit this rapid success.

THE MARIANAS

Both sides knew that the seizure of the Marianas by American forces would be a turning point in the war. Japan's Home Islands would be within range of American heavy bombers.

At Tarawa and in the Marshall Islands, the islands' size prevented the defenders from preparing deeply entrenched lines of resistance. The topography of the larger islands in the Marianas chain allowed a better in-depth defensive system.

However, the sudden appearance of the Americans in the Marianas prevented the Japanese from establishing strong lines of resistance and exploiting the terrain on the three main islands of Saipan, Tinian, and Guam.

PELELIU

The island of Peleliu in the Palau Islands was not supposed to be part of Nimitz's Central Pacific drive. But by mid-1944, American planners declared that this island hosting an airfield was to be seized to protect the Southwest Pacific Drive, now reaching the Philippines.

At Peleliu and in the later campaigns, however, the Japanese built and used complex underground fortifications and mutually supported lines of resistance that made the Pacific War even more costly in human lives for the Americans.

THE COMBATANTS

BETIO (TARAWA)

At just over half a square mile, Betio was the largest island of the chain forming the atoll of Tarawa in the Gilbert Islands. It fell to the Imperial Japanese Navy to organize its defense and fortification. On Betio, the Japanese built an airfield and a series of formidable defenses (pillboxes, gun emplacements, etc.) that would defeat the Americans on the island's shoreline. An almost continuous seawall made of coconut tree logs was built around the island to prevent American vehicles from advancing inland.

The island's garrison, the 3rd Special Base Unit, was under Rear Admiral Keiji Shibazaki's command. Attached to this unit were the pioneers of the 111th Construction Battalion, the 4th Construction Unit, and the Rikusentai of the 7th Sasebo Special Naval Landing Forces (SNLF), totaling about 5,000 men, of which 1,400 were Korean conscripts.

The island's mobile defense was provided by the Tank Unit, 3rd Special Base Unit (14 Type 95 light tanks). Two platoons, one of three tanks and the other of two, were detached to the 7th SNLF in support of the 2nd and 3rd companies respectively.

Petty Officer Tadao Onuki had been a truck driver during the early Japanese campaigns in China and Indochina. Seeking further action, he volunteered to join a tank outfit in the Pacific. Upon arriving on Betio, he was assigned as a Ha-Go tank commander in the Tank Unit, 3rd Special Base Unit.

Tank maintenance and resupply on the island was poor, especially since the Americans began daily bombings on Betio prior to the invasion.

Some of the garrison tanks were hidden in prepared revetments dug into the ground to act as pillboxes, but most were kept "in the open" to counterattack the

American beachhead on D-Day. This situation resulted in casualties among vehicles and tank crews from the American preparatory naval gunfire.

Marines from the 2nd Division were designated to take Tarawa. Two Regimental Combat Teams, the 2nd and 8th Marines, would form the assault force to take Betio, totaling barely over 10,000 men. The remaining regiment, the 6th Marines, was retained as the Corps Reserve, to be deployed in case of absolute necessity. Engineers and artillerymen supported the infantry battalions. Carrier-based aircraft and destroyers' 16in. guns provided fire support to the attackers.

A natural obstacle forced the Americans to convert amphibian tractors, originally employed as logistic vehicles, into tactical assault vehicles. A fringing reef prevented most Navy landing craft from delivering troops ashore at low tide. In total, 125 Landing Vehicles Tracked (LVTs) were thus

Japanese tankmen are checking the Type 97 machine gun from one of their Chi-Ha medium tanks. The armored cover is still in place around the gun barrel. Note the empty ammunition collector bag still attached to the machine gun. (Akira Takizawa)

used to carry the first three assault waves to the shore. The other two were carried by landing craft, the famous LCVPs (Landing Craft Vehicle Personnel).

Two light tank companies from the 2nd Tank Battalion, reinforced by a medium tank company, were attached to the division's Regimental Combat Teams.

While still stationed in New Caledonia, 1st Lieutenant Edward L. Bale Jr's C Company, 1st Corps Tank Battalion (medium) was selected to land at Tarawa. This separate tank battalion was activated to provide individual companies to infantry divisions, to support their organic light tank companies in operation.

Bale was one of the few men in the company to have experience in the Marine Corps. Before he took over the company, he commanded a tank platoon from the 51st Composite Defense Battalion, a segregated unit with white officers and black enlisted men. When the tank platoon was disbanded, Bale asked to be transferred to the new medium tank battalion. As the senior officer in the battalion, he took over C Company.

Other men within the company were inexperienced, and many had joined the Marine Corps because they were about to be drafted. Marines had become acquainted with tanks (M3s, M4A4s, and M4A2s) at Camp Pendleton on the American west coast. Officers were taught about the employment of tanks in combat at Fort Knox. At that time, the US Army emphasized large attacks by armored formations, inspired by the Germans' blitzkrieg in Europe. Bale recalled:

This business of going out front and running around and cruising and all, that all got started with the Army [at Fort Knox] … [Cruise] was the term that was used for running

The crew of Cecilia poses for the camera sometime before shipping out to the South Pacific. Standing from left to right: Private First Class Asard Zeibak (assistant driver), Sergeant Robert M. Keller (tank commander), Sergeant Michael E. Shivetts (radio/loader). Kneeling is Corporal Alfonso A. Chavez (driver) whose newborn daughter was named Cecilia, hence the tank name. At Tarawa, the tank was commanded by 1st Lieutenant Edward L. Bale Jr and Keller became the assistant driver. These men would be the first USMC tankers to be involved in a tank duel with the enemy. (Michael E. Shivetts)

around on the objective. That was a tactic that the Army taught. I don't know whether it came from the horse cavalry running over a hill and riding around on the hilltop, or what the hell it came from.

But Marine tank officers were as green as the men they commanded and couldn't foresee that the doctrine they had been taught might be unsuited to war in the Pacific. A tank gunner in the company recalled:

Our instructions [given by the officers] were "You drive across the island, don't even bother to shoot or nothing." Instructions were to push across the island as quickly as possible and return, firing only as necessary, turn around and come back. Then if you happened to see something, shoot it.

When the company departed from the US in July 1943, it was equipped with 14 brand-new medium tank M4A2s. The company was organized around three platoons of four tanks each plus a Headquarters Section with two tanks.

When arriving in New Caledonia, "there was no place that you could train [with tanks] and when we weren't doing maintenance it was hikes," recalled a member of the company.

As a matter of fact, the company was able to maneuver its tanks only during two rehearsals prior to the landing at Tarawa. In both cases, tanks were landed behind the infantry and stopped on the beach. At no point did tanks train with infantry. The sole tank–infantry coordination was carried out by a unit of reconnaissance guides (within the company itself) who were trained to walk in front of the tanks to guide them around shell holes on the reef.

USMC M4A2 TURRET

1. Commander's hatch
2. Pistol port
3. Gunner's seat
4. .50-cal. machine-gun barrel
5. Gunner's periscope
6. Telescope
7. Gyrostabilizer control box
8. 75mm gun and .30-cal. MG foot firing switches
9. Loader's periscope
10. .30-cal. machine gun
11. 75mm M3 main gun
12. Turret manual traversing mechanism

To make things worse, planners put their trust in the preliminary naval bombardment. Sergeant Michael E. Shivetts, the loader in the command tank, recalled: "[Aboard ship] we had been told the island would be sunk by naval gunfire, so I wasn't worried about being killed or getting hit. Big mistake."

When the tanks of C Company landed on the reef at Betio, "we hadn't fired a gun since we began to move out of Pendleton," said Bale.

ENIWETOK (MARSHALL ISLANDS)

The defense of Eniwetok Atoll was organized around the 1st Amphibious Brigade of the Imperial Japanese Army, commanded by Major-General Nishida Yoshimi. In total,

41

The tank–infantry telephone mounted on the rear of all tanks after the Marshall Islands campaign greatly improved coordination. Here, a rifleman guides Circle 3 from the Tank Company, 4th Marines through densely vegetated terrain on Guam. (NARA)

3,500 men defended the island of Eniwetok, 1,365 defended Parry, and 1,250 Engebi. The islands' defenses were less impressive than those of Tarawa, though several well-positioned pillboxes containing machine guns and antitank guns represented an obvious threat.

Nine Ha-Gos of the Tank Unit, 1st Sea-Mobile Brigade, attached to the 1st Amphibious Brigade, were equally divided among the three islands. The Type 95s were dug into the ground to prevent detection. They would be used as pillboxes to repulse an enemy landing. An opening in the entrenchment allowed the tank to leave its shelter to charge in the direction of an enemy beachhead.

The atoll of Eniwetok would be attacked by a mixed Marine Corps–Army brigade-sized force, with its own supporting units (engineers, medical, ordnance, reconnaissance units, etc.). It was built around the 22nd Marines and Army's 106th Regiment, totaling about 10,000 personnel for the assault.

The 22nd Marines was supported by an independent tank unit, the 2nd Separate Tank Company with 16 vehicles.

Like at Tarawa, many of the tank crews had never before experienced combat. Robert Meier was 16 when he joined the company in Samoa. He was selected to serve on tanks—then light M3A1s: "I got in them and right away they picked me as a gunner because I had good eyes."

The unit was issued medium tanks only six weeks before shipping out to the Marshall Islands.

Of the company's 15 M4A2s, six were refurbished vehicles from the old C Company, 1st Corps Tank Battalion that had seen combat on Tarawa. The sixteenth vehicle was the company tank recovery vehicle, a retriever based on a Sherman chassis.

Though inexperienced, news from the Tarawa operations and the near disaster had reached the tank company. Thus, the tanks were equipped with homemade wading stacks, a microphone was put on the rear of each vehicle for infantry to communicate with the crew, and anti-magnetic mine revetments were put on the tanks' hulls. Little training was undertaken with infantry because of the lack of time.

SAIPAN AND TINIAN

The defense of the Marianas was under Lieutenant-General Obata Hideyoshi, IJA, commander of the 31st Army. The island of Saipan was defended by the 135th and 136th Infantry regiments, the 5th Special Base Force of the IJA (collectively making up three-quarters of the strength), and by the 55th Guard Force and the Yokosuka 1st Special Base Force from the IJN (the remaining quarter of the strength), totaling some 31,500 men.

The Tank Unit of the 55th Guard Force (IJN) and the 9th Tank Regiment (IJA) would provide the mobile counterattack force in case of an American landing. The 9th Tank Regiment was a mixed regiment of light and medium tanks. This regiment had been activated in Manchuria in 1942 as part of the 2nd Tank Brigade, 1st Tank Division in view of occupying positions along the northern Manchurian border. But in March 1944, the regiment was detached and sent to the Marianas to improve the now-vulnerable Japanese possessions. Two of the six regiments' tank companies were sent to Guam, while others were kept on Saipan, as was the Maintenance Company.

This Ha-Go, knocked out on a road on Saipan, shows bamboo poles mounted on the back for infantrymen to hold onto while the tank was moving. The unprotected tank riders (foreground) were usually the first victims of the powerful American fire. (MCHD)

Table 5: 9th Tank Regiment (IJA)					
9th Tank Regiment	Commander	Type 95 Ha-Go	Type 97 Chi-Ha	Type 97 Shinhoto Chi-Ha	Location
HQ Company	Colonel Masa Goshima	3	1	1	Saipan
1st Company	Lieutenant Sekimi Yuki	17	0	0	Guam
2nd Company	Captain Tsunenari Sato	3	10	1	Guam
3rd Company	Captain Norio Nishidate	3	10	1	Saipan
4th Company	Captain Nario Yoshimura	3	10	1	Saipan
5th Company	Captain Katufumi Shibata	3	10	1	Saipan
Maintenance Company	Lieutenant Mamoru Torikai	0	0	0	Saipan

The Japanese 9th Tank Regiment was composed of a mixture of tank models, such as this Type 95 Ha-Go (left) and Type 97 Chi-Ha (right), both knocked out on Saipan, June 17, 1944. (NARA)

American assault forces consisted of the 2nd and 4th Marine divisions and the Army's 27th Infantry Division. Each Marine division brought its organic tank battalion. The 4th Tank Battalion was a veteran of combat on the islands of Kwajalein Atoll in the Marshall Islands, while the 2nd Tank Battalion had seen its share of combat in the Solomons and at Tarawa. The Marine Corps did not need individual medium tank companies anymore since it was converting to all-medium tank battalions.

During training, tank–infantry cooperation was greatly improved with the addition of a telephone to the rear of each tank so the infantry could better control tanks. In addition, jeeps were equipped with TCS radios for tank company commanders to better coordinate tank attacks with infantry at battalion level.

Better coordination with supporting arms (artillery, aviation, and naval gunfire) was also emphasized. To prevent friendly fire, large markings were painted on the tank turret tops. The 4th Tank Battalion painted the turret tops in yellow while the 2nd Tank Battalion painted large white five-pointed stars. This was to help aerial observers to better locate the front lines and thus adjust gunfire support. This time, factory-designed wading stacks were available to all tanks.

After Tarawa, Bale's company was re-designated A Company, 2nd Tank Battalion. He recalled:

> Probably some of the best combined arms training I've ever been through took place [in Hawaii] in the Second Marine Division. I attributed it to several things. We had lost so many people and learned so many lessons following Tarawa, and we didn't know where we were going, but we wanted to apply all those things and did not want to make the mistakes, and did not want to lose the lives. Before the division embarked and left there, the division staff laid out on the ground, using a chalk line, and said "this is the beach, and over here is something else, and over here is a road" and this kind of thing. It duplicated where we were going to land. Then everybody walked through it. Didn't make any difference whether you were in tanks or the artillery or what, you walked through it. I've often said, I didn't say it today because I have friends out in that audience, and also panelists who would disagree violently with me, but I also think that—and I've served in four Marine Divisions at one time or another between World War II and Korea and Viet Nam—the 2nd Marine Division when it left Hawaii going to Saipan was probably the best trained Marine Division I've ever seen.

Private First Class Robert U. Falkenbury, a tank crew member in C Company, 2nd Tank Battalion was a veteran of the Tarawa operation. His company, then equipped with light tanks M3A1s, was about to be issued new M4A2 Shermans. He and several other men in the company were selected to pick up the new vehicles at the depot in Hawaii. Among the tanks parked there, a handful of new M4A2s of the later model (with a single glacis plate and large hatches) was available. Having been through combat, he and his fellow tankers knew the importance of having large hatches to facilitate leaving a flooding or burning tank under fire. These vehicles were always first choice. The rest, to reach the authorized amount of tanks, was made up of mid-production M4A2s.

TYPE 95 HA-GO TURRET

1. Vision slit
2. Asbestos panel
3. Turret traverse handle
4. Type 94 main gun breech
5. Bag for collecting empty shell cases
6. Leather pad rest
7. Main gun ammunition ready rack
8. Turret-mounted 7.7mm Type 97 machine gun
9. Machine-gun sight
10. Bag for collecting empty bullet cases
11. Main gun sight

Each of the three medium tank companies within the 2nd Tank Battalion was equipped with 15 M4A2s.[8] One of them was equipped with a bulldozer blade to seal caves and deal with beach obstacles. Only one retriever was available at battalion level. An additional fourth tank company was equipped with M3A1s converted to flame-thrower tanks to deal with entrenched Japanese positions and M5A1s for command purposes. A Headquarters and Service (H&S) Company filled administrative and ordnance duties. The 4th Tank Battalion was built on a similar basis.

After Saipan was declared secure, these Marine units would attack Tinian, in a shore-to-shore landing. The main body of the defenders on Tinian were the IJA 50th Infantry Regiment, 29th Division supported by 12 Type 95 Ha-Gos of the Tank Unit, 18th Infantry Regiment, 29th Division and the IJN 56th Guard Force, totaling about 8,000 men.

---

8   Marine tank battalions were officially authorized 14 medium tanks per company at the time.

GUAM

The defense of Guam was organized around 11,500 men from the IJA. These were mainly from the 29th Division's 38th and 18th regiments, the 48th Independent Mixed Brigade (IMB), and the 10th Independent Mixed Regiment.

The detached 1st Company, 9th Tank Regiment was attached to the 38th Regiment while the 2nd Company, 9th Tank Regiment was attached to the 48th IMB. The 29th Division's Tank Unit had only nine Ha-Gos out of 17 that safely reached Guam prior to the American attack. The other eight Type 95s were sunk aboard their transport en route to the Marianas on February 29, 1944 by an American submarine.

Captain Hideo Sato was designated as the new Commanding Officer of the Tank Unit, 29th Division right before the unit shipped out of Korea on February 24, 1944. He graduated from the officers' course at Chiba Tank School in 1940. The course lasted from four to six months and was equally divided between practical and tactical tank employment. There, Sato studied each individual tank an armored division could be equipped with, the position and role of each crew member, and the maintenance of these vehicles. Little time was devoted to the study of Soviet tank characteristics. Strategy and tactics were mostly theoretical. They lacked experienced instructors and, worse, connection with field units. As a result, students like Sato were given instruction which "presupposes the existence of equipment which the armored divisions and other independent units not only do not possess but have little prospect of obtaining." Thus,

After the Marshall Islands campaign, Marine Corps tank units were issued one tank dozer per company. Here, the Tank Company, 4th Marines dozer tank clears destroyed Ha-Gos off the road to Sumay, Guam in 1944. (NARA)

Marines from the Tank Company, 4th Marines take cover from a hidden sniper on Guam. Beside the two tanks from 2nd Platoon is one of the four jeeps the company had equipped with a TCS radio. This radio was compatible with the GF/RU radio installed in tanks and allowed the company commander to coordinate attacks from a jeep. This permitted better coordination in a combined attack rather than commanding from inside a tank. (MCHD)

when Sato joined the 6th Tank Regiment in Manchuria in March 1940, he realized he could not apply the tactics learned at Chiba, owing to the lack of specialized equipment such as armored personnel carriers or tank destroyers. He gained experience practicing in the field until he was promoted in February 1944 as the Commanding Officer of the 29th Division Tank Unit.

The 38,500 men from the USMC 3rd Division and 1st Provisional Brigade and Army 77th Infantry Division would seize Guam. The 3rd Marine Division was supported by its organic tank battalion, fielding 46 tanks within three tank companies (see Table 6). Six M4A2s were equipped with E4-5 mechanized flame-throwers. The weapon was operated by the bow gunner, in place of the hull machine gun. Command, logistics, and supply would be organized by H&S Company.

In total, 35 more tanks from two tank companies were attached to the two rifle regiments of the 1st Provisional Marine Brigade.

The former 2nd Separate Tank Company that fought on Eniwetok was redesignated Tank Company, 22nd Marines and was now definitively attached to this regiment.

The Tank Company, 4th Marines was also an experienced unit since it had participated in the Bougainville operation in 1943 as A Company, 3rd Tank Battalion and was detached from its mother battalion to support the 4th Marines in the assault on Emirau in 1944. When the 1st Provisional Marine Brigade formed up on Guadalcanal in March 1944, the unit was re-designated Tank Company, 4th Marines and was permanently attached to this unit from then on.

Like the 2nd Tank Battalion, all tanks were thoroughly waterproofed and equipped with fording kits prior to the attack on Guam. But only a handful of factory-made wading stacks reached the tank companies. As a result, the 3rd Tank Battalion and 4th Marines' Tank Company designed their own using 55gal empty fuel drums. The Tank Company, 22nd Marines designed the stack roots, but were issued factory-made upper parts and adapted them on the tanks.

All tanks were equipped with tank–infantry telephones for communication, and training between both was greatly emphasized while on Guadalcanal prior to the assault.

Table 6: US Marines tank support on Guam					
3rd Tank Battalion				**1st Provisional Marine Brigade**	
H&S Company	A Company	B Company	C Company	Tank Company, 4th Marines	Tank Company, 22nd Marines
1 tank	14 tanks	14 tanks (x 3 w/E4-5)	14 tanks (x 3 w/E4-5)	17 tanks	16 tanks
	1 dozer tank	1 dozer tank	1 dozer tank	1 dozer tank	1 dozer tank
	1 retriever	1 retriever	1 retriever	1 retriever	1 retriever

PELELIU

The island of Peleliu was defended by some 13,000 IJA soldiers from the experienced 14th Division commanded by Lieutenant-General Inoue Sadao. Some 15,000 other IJN and IJA troops as well as 10,000 laborers constructed in-depth fortifications in the hilly center of the island. Mobile defense was provided by 17 Type 95s from the Tank Unit, 14th Division.

Private First Class Shu Kin was a mechanic in the Maintenance Platoon, 14th Division Tank Unit. He was conscripted into the IJA at 22 and assigned to the 1st Cavalry Regiment, 1st Division. After about two years of training, formation, and duties in Japan and Manchuria, he was transferred to the 14th Division Tank Unit in February 1944. By mid-March, the unit left Manchuria for the Palaus after a series of stops in Japan and Guam. Kin and his unit reached Peleliu in July 1944.

The company-size unit was built around a command section, three tank platoons, and a maintenance platoon as shown in the organization chart shown overleaf. During the preliminary American bombardment, tanks were sheltered in caves, but trucks, used to resupply tanks, were parked in the open and were all destroyed.

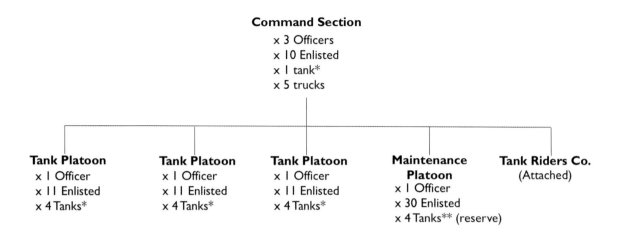

Command Section
x 3 Officers
x 10 Enlisted
x 1 tank*
x 5 trucks

Tank Platoon
x 1 Officer
x 11 Enlisted
x 4 Tanks*

Tank Platoon
x 1 Officer
x 11 Enlisted
x 4 Tanks*

Tank Platoon
x 1 Officer
x 11 Enlisted
x 4 Tanks*

Maintenance Platoon
x 1 Officer
x 30 Enlisted
x 4 Tanks** (reserve)

Tank Riders Co.
(Attached)

* Kin stated that the company commander's and platoon leader's tanks were equipped with "key-radios" to communicate with each other. The nature of these radios is unknown.
** One tank was fitted with a "special towing hook" at the rear end to be used as a retriever.

A company of tank riders was also attached to the Tank Unit. These troops were trained to ride on the outside of the tanks, on a platform attached to the rear of the vehicle. Three men would be assigned to a light tank (five to a medium). If enemy vehicles were encountered, tank riders were to disembark when small-arms fire hit the tank in order to knock out enemy vehicles with mines and grenades.

The American new 81st Infantry Division and the old 1st Marine Division and its organic tank battalion, veteran of the Solomon Islands campaign, were designated to take Peleliu.

The tank company structure was modified after the Marianas campaign. Each platoon was reduced to three tanks and an additional platoon was allotted. An additional vehicle was also authorized within Headquarters, making a theoretical total of five platoons of three tanks each per company.

The lack of specialized transport ships, however, prevented transport of the entire 1st Tank Battalion. Instead, only the 15 tanks of A Company and its retriever, nine tanks from B Company, and six tanks from C Company were taken to Peleliu.

Moreover, the M4A2s were issued only seven weeks prior to embarkation, and 60 percent of the replacement personnel within the battalion originated from infantry units and arrived only two months before the operation.

The short period of time devoted to training was focused on familiarization with the new vehicles and tank–infantry cooperation. Now a standard practice within Marine tank units, tank–infantry telephones were added to the rear of each tank for better coordination. Tank armor was increased by welding track links to the turret sides and front slope of each vehicle to protect against antitank weapons. The E4-5 flame-thrower was standardized after Guam: eight of these weapons were issued to each company.

A total of 47,500 US assault troops would land on Peleliu.

COMBAT

TARAWA

On the morning of November 20, 1943, the fourth assault wave carrying the 14 medium tanks from C Company, 1st Corps Tank Battalion (medium) approached the reef. The previous waves of infantry were pinned on the beach, unable to move inland.

Underwater shell holes proved deadly to many M4A2s at Tarawa. Cecilia fell victim to one of these craters on November 21 while attacking a fortified position along the beach. The result of its encounter with a Ha-Go is clearly visible on the muzzle of the main gun. (NARA)

This is most likely the Type 95 that disabled Cecilia's gun on D-Day at Tarawa. Note the holes on the left-hand side of the hull made by the 75mm main gun of the M4A2 Commando. This is an early model, as indicated by the short fenders and the absence of the reinforced ring around the commander's cupola. (NMPW)

On Red Beach One, in the early afternoon hours, only the two Headquarters tanks from 1st Lieutenant Edward L. Bale Jr's company were able to cross the seawall. The other four tanks from 1st Platoon fell victim to underwater shell holes on the reef or sustained mechanical failures.

Lieutenant Bale was riding in his command tank, Cecilia, named after the driver's newborn daughter. As he penetrated inland, Bale immediately tried to establish contact with the 3rd Battalion, 2nd Marines (3/2) but was unable to locate the survivors.[9] "We didn't see any Marines. We saw a lot of Japanese running, and we started shooting at them with the machine guns." American tanks were progressing behind Green Beach and began reducing enemy positions facing the sea. "We were attacking them from the rear," recalled Bale, "we fired into this [140mm coastal defense gun]."

Unknown to him, the survivors from the 3/2 reorganized themselves and put together three companies that followed both M4A2s, about 50yd behind.

At some point, Cecilia outdistanced the other Sherman, Commando. Both tanks disappeared in the dust and smoke raised by the preliminary bombardment, ahead of the infantry.

---

9   All Marine regiments regardless of type are referred to as "2nd Marines," etc., omitting the word regiment.

At training, tanks always progressed guided by reconnaissance men on foot, who pointed out unseen obstacles and enemy positions. At that point of the battle, none of them had caught up with the tanks' advance off the beach. Drivers made extensive use of the steering brakes to slalom around debris, but about 200yd inland, Cecilia got stuck on coconut logs. Michael E. Shivetts, the radio operator and loader in Cecilia, recalled: "That was our downfall. Coconut logs. We got stuck on coconut logs. Chavez, our driver, he had that job because he was the best driver in the company— good enough that Ed Bale rode with him. We got hung up on coconut logs and that's when we got knocked out of action."

Ed Bale recalled: "Suddenly a Japanese tank turret crops up over a revetment. They had a little 37mm gun that had a shoulder harness type thing that they elevated and depressed the gun with. So, I had my gunner [Charles E. Martin] take a shot at him." The turret was rotated 30° to the right when Martin, excited, fired and, "He missed. The Japanese fired. His 37mm round hit the end of the gun tube [of Cecilia] and a big piece of his armor piercing projectile came down the tube, ruined the gun tube."

After destroying a Ha-Go on Tarawa, Commando forged ahead of the infantry, and was finally destroyed by hidden Japanese antitank guns. At short range, the Type 94 antitank gun was able to penetrate the side armor of the Sherman. (NMPW)

Shivetts was ready to feed the breech with another round: "The thirty-seven millimeter [round] entered the tube of the gun … and blew out the gun about six to eight inches down [the bore]. Unfortunately the breech was open, I'm sitting there with a seventy-five millimeter in my lap. There was a flash came through." Fragments and sparks filled the turret. "The thing lit up like a Christmas tree, seven or eight

different colors … I think it was Ed hollered something about flashback. Not being a tank man but a radio man I hollered back 'Flashback my ass, something hit me!' It was a piece of shrapnel, and hit me. Lucky as hell that there was no seventy-five millimeter in that breech of the gun. The breech was open."[10]

Commando finally closed the distance with Cecilia and fired several 75mm rounds at the Type 95, blowing its turret up in the air and ending the duel.

After about 45 minutes, Chavez managed to extricate the tank out of its trap. Bale recounted: "I radioed over that I was going back to the beach and I went back to the beach [guided by recon guide James W. Tobey] because I was scared to fire any ammunition down that gun tube. Got back, took one look down it, and I said 'This tank has now become a mobile machine gun.' We went back in and worked with the infantry acting as a mobile machine gun."

With the turret traverse mechanism also damaged, the tank was mainly used to haul water and ammunition to the infantry during the rest of the afternoon.

Commando forged ahead, followed by infantry, and was credited with the destruction of two 5in. anti-boat guns and five pillboxes. Arriving near the southwestern tip of the island, Commando was fired at by between one and four 37mm Type 94 guns at point-blank range (less than 200yd).

The tank was hit 18 times and several rounds penetrated the right sponson armor, ending all tank support in the Red Beach One/Green Beach sector. Miraculously, the whole crew made it out safely, back to the beach.

By 1630hrs, the 3/2 commander decided to fall back to defend a smaller perimeter during the night.

Despite the heavy losses and disorganization, Marine infantry and tankers quickly learned from their mistakes. The two surviving medium tanks on the island were

---

10 A flashback occurred when unburned propellant remained smoldering in the gun tube. When the breech was opened, air rushed in and the propellant ignited, sending a flash of fire out of the breech.

carefully protected, and both infantry and tanks worked in close coordination to secure Betio after 72 hours of tough fighting.

ENIWETOK

The first island to be assaulted in the Eniwetok Atoll chain was Engebi. The 22nd Marines landed on the southwestern shore of the island at 0845hrs on the morning of February 18, 1944. The 15 M4A2s of the 2nd Separate Tank Company landed with the fourth wave at 0900hrs.

In the 2/22 zone, on Blue Beach Three, despite the disorganization, infantry progressed rapidly to the airfield. There, the Marines stopped to let the artillery barrage reduce Japanese opposition in the airfield's vicinity. The 2nd Platoon from the 2nd Separate Tank Company, attached to the 2/22, reached the infantry in the area.

At that point, dug-in Japanese Type 95 Ha-Gos were spotted by infantry. The three Japanese tanks on the island were entrenched and used as pillboxes to ambush the attackers. Infantry communicated the targets to the tankers thanks to a transmitter fitted at the back of the tanks, a major improvement in tank–infantry communications.[11] With their 75mm guns, the American tanks blasted their opponents apart in a few minutes.

11 The transmitter was most probably a microphone similar to that carried inside the tanks.

Entrenched vehicles used as pillboxes were difficult to locate. This Type 95 was destroyed by M4A2s of the 2nd Separate Tank Company on Engebi on February 15, 1944. (NARA)

Infantry was able to cross the airfield, and by mid-morning had secured most of its objective. The island was declared secure by 1450hrs. Tanks re-embarked aboard LCMs by mid-afternoon for their next operation. Maintenance and rearming were carried out afloat during the night, aboard the LCMs tied alongside their mother ship, the LSD-1 (Landing Ship Dock) USS *Ashland*.

Eniwetok Island lies some 25 miles south of Engebi, across the lagoon. It was assaulted by the Army's 106th Infantry Regiment on the morning of February 19.

Captain Harry Calcutt volunteered his tank company to support the Army in this assault. Y-Hour was postponed twice to give time to the LCMs carrying the M4A2s from the 2nd Separate Tank Company to cross the lagoon. "The Army got tied down on the beach right away … And we kind of rescued them," recalled Robert Meier, from HQ Platoon. With the help of Calcutt's tanks, the infantry got off the beach and progressed inland. The three dug-in Type 95s on the island were all destroyed either by infantry or the preliminary bombardment. The island was finally secured by the end of the day with the help of the 22nd Marines coming from Engebi. The 2nd Separate Tank Company vehicles were backloaded aboard the LSD the next day.

Maintenance was carried out aboard the LSD on February 21. Meier explained: "We had to go down [to the well deck] and service our tanks. Fuel them and clean the guns and do all of that while we're aboard ship."

The last objective of the atoll was Parry, three miles north of Eniwetok Island. On February 22, the battered 22nd Marines landed at Parry in three waves. The Green Beach Three sector was tenaciously defended by Japanese troops, who inflicted serious

Circle 2 Cobra was temporarily disabled by an underwater shell hole on Eniwetok Island, while supporting US Army troops from the 106th Infantry Regiment. (NARA)

casualties on the 1/22. When tanks landed, they immediately proceeded westward accompanied by infantry.

In the 1/22 zone, a composite platoon of four Shermans was leading the advance. As they paused to wait for the accompanying infantry to join them, three Type 95 Ha-Gos from the Tank Company, 1st Sea-Mobile Brigade left their entrenchments and charged in the direction of the American medium tanks.

The Ha-Gos fired first and scored direct hits on Shirley with their 37mm guns, without disabling the M4A2. The American tanks fired back with all their guns. In Circle 2 Cobra, Private First Class Frank Bulan, the gunner, fired three rounds at one of the enemy tanks.[12] Sergeant George Ryan was watching through his periscope: "When we hit the Jap tank, the turret rose right up off it so we could see daylight under it." Shirley and Caesar took care of the other two Ha-Gos within several minutes.

In Triangle 3, Meier could see "a bunch of Japs down there running in a column of trees … and all of a sudden we hear this heavy fire. We thought it was mortars. We thought the Japs were shooting mortars at us … We started moving around … We didn't know at that time it was naval gunfire, but it was … And they hit two of our tanks."

During the landing, the first wave of the 1/22 hit south of their assigned beach. Unaware of this, the battalion commander requested naval gunfire in an area where he expected troops to be absent. Five salvoes fell among the Marine armor and infantry.

The result was devastating. Diamond 4 Caesar was hit twice, killing one crew

---

12 Several Marine tank companies were still using an old prewar tactical marking system under which tanks from the platoons were marked with geometric symbols.

Associated Press correspondent Al Dopking (right) chatting with men from the 2nd Separate Tank Company after the battle on Parry Island, Eniwetok Atoll. In the background, the turret of the M4A2 Shirley shows the scar left by a 37mm AP round fired by one of the three Ha-Gos that charged the beachhead. (NARA)

member and wounding three others.[13] "The other one caught on fire, they got knocked out. Everybody got out of the tank ok [through the escape hatch]. But that engine compartment took a shell … big five-inch shell [knocking out both engines] … That's what they were shooting at us." Meier's tank, as well as Shirley, were not hit.

Miraculously, only ten Marine infantrymen were wounded. The bitter report of Captain Calcutt stated:

> Five-inch guns will penetrate the two-inch armor of medium tanks and generally raise hell with them. We would appreciate it if they would call their gunfire somewhere else, especially when we are forced to hold the tanks static in the gunfire in order to cover the infantry in the same area in an attempt to silence what we thought to be enemy opposition.

Despite the violence, the Marines quickly recovered and resumed their advance to the west coast, and then to the south.

---

13 This is the official casualty count. According to Robert Meier, the whole crew was killed instantly.

The island was declared secure by 1945hrs, though several Japanese troops were still holding the southern tip of the island, taken the next morning.

An officer from the 22nd Marines commented: "If [the Japanese tanks] had attacked the infantry before tank support arrived, the battle for Parry Island would have been very bloody indeed."

SAIPAN AND TINIAN

This still from a combat film shows the results of a 16in. shell fired by supporting US Navy battleships on Diamond 4 Caesar. The round probably bounced on the ground before hitting the tank. A direct hit would have disintegrated the Sherman. (NARA)

Marines landed on Saipan on June 15, 1944. Despite heavy casualties in men and material, the two Marine divisions achieved strong beachheads and began penetrating inland.

In the 2nd Division zone, north of the town of Charan Kanoa, the 6th Marines were a few yards away from the day's objective. They had captured the radio station on D-Day and spent the following day consolidating gains and repulsing a first Japanese tank–infantry counterattack. The IJN and 4th Company, 9th Tank Regiment vehicles were destroyed by infantry weapons.

On June 16, the Japanese managed to organize another counterattack on the 6th Marines perimeter. They designated the radio station, located some 400yd behind the 6th Marines line, as the first objective. The remaining tank companies of the 9th Tank Regiment formed the spearhead of this attack, coordinated with some 1,000 infantry from the 136th Infantry Regiment and the 1st Yokosuka Special Naval Landing Force.

Aerial observers spotted enemy tanks north of the 2nd Division perimeter and radioed ground troops to expect a tank attack during the night.

Marines gathered 37mm antitank guns, mortars, 50-cal. machine guns and 2.36in. rocket launchers ("bazookas") on the front line. Weapons Company SPM half-tracks mounting 75mm guns were positioned right behind the first line, as well as tanks from 1st Platoon, B Company, 2nd Tank Battalion. They were to be used in case of absolute necessity.

In the early hours of June 17, 1944, 31 Japanese tanks started their engines and headed for the 6th Marines perimeter. At about 0330hrs, 1/6 outposts heard the roaring of tank engines and the clanking of tank tracks in the dark. By 0345hrs, the first Japanese tanks hit the 1/6 line.

Sergeant Shiro Shimoda was a bow gunner in a Type 95 Ha-Go from HQ Platoon, 3rd Company, 9th Tank Regiment:

Countless tracers and star shells were lighting up the night sky like daytime; red streaks of enemy tracers were flying directly at us as if they were waiting for our tanks.

We had to advance in two columns due to the rough terrain. Usually the line

In the early hours of June 17, 1944, the Japanese launched a large night tank attack on American lines at Saipan. This Ha-Go from the 5th Company, 9th Tank Regiment, probably a survivor of this attack, was later put out of action by bazooka fire in the hilly terrain. Note the spare track links on the front left fender. (P.G. and Mark Navarro)

formation was used for the attack, but we were forced to advance in a disadvantageous formation. Our tanks rumbled down the ridge and dashed into the enemy positions.

All Marine infantry weapons were brought to bear on the attacking tanks. Some infantry from the 136th Infantry Regiment were riding on the tanks' engine decks. They were the first victims of the deadly American fire. But the Japanese tanks kept coming. Shimoda recalled:

"Fire into the sky!", shouted SgtMaj Nakao, my tank commander. Because of the column formation, shooting forwards would damage a friendly tank; so he told us to fire into the sky, to frighten the enemy with our tracers. I aimed my machine gun upwards and pulled the trigger. SgtMaj Nakao was loading a round into the main gun. Most of the infantrymen on our tanks were killed or simply abandoned us. Due to the unusual column attack, tanks were disordered and the chain-of-command ceased to exist. The leading parts of the columns advanced deeply and a confused fight developed. I was only pulling the trigger unconsciously. Star shells were lighting up our tanks and American gun and bazooka fires were destroying them.

"Many of the tanks were unbuttoned, the crew chief directing from the top of his open turret. Some were being led by a crew member afoot," wrote Major James A. Donovan, 1/6 Executive Officer. The main blow fell upon the men of B/1/6. "By this time, the whole company position had been penetrated by the tanks and the battle evolved into a madhouse of noise, tracers, and flashing lights."

As Japanese tanks were hit by infantry weapons, they caught fire and silhouetted other tanks. Shimoda's Type 95 had penetrated as far as the tank platoon from B Company, 2nd Tank Battalion, some 300yd behind the infantry line:

American M4 Sherman tanks suddenly appeared and we opened fire on them, but our shells bounced off them like baseballs owing to their thick armor. Tanks of 9th Tank Regiment were destroyed one after another, bursting into flames and burning with billowing smoke. The few surviving infantrymen had also fallen by now. My tank was passing the company commander's tank when it was hit; red flames burst out, and no one escaped—[Captain] Nishidate and his crew were all killed immediately.

In the darkness, Shimoda's tank was hit and had to be abandoned by its crew, who fought on foot from then on. Shimoda continued:

At the first gray of dawn the sounds of firing dwindled and the results of the fight became clear. It was an appalling sight to see the smoldering wrecks of 24 tanks scattered across the battlefield. SgtMaj Nakao ordered us to withdraw to the company HQ at Chacha. While we were crawling up the rocky mountainside trying to find our way back to the HQ, Nishida's lone tank passed us, heading to the rear. He stopped the tank at the ridge and shouted, "All our friends were annihilated!" It was the end of the 9th Tank Regiment.

This was also the end of the largest Japanese tank attack of the Pacific War. In the aftermath, Americans counted some 24 wrecked Japanese tanks in and ahead of their lines, and some 700 dead Japanese soldiers and sailors. After the fight, many units claimed the destruction of the Japanese tank force that night. Ed Bale explained: "The argument has never been settled who destroyed the Japanese tanks, whether B Company, [2nd] Tank Battalion did or whether the Weapons Company, 6th Marines did. Anybody that's still living is arguing over it."

The crew of C30 C.O.D. destroyed five Japanese tanks within the space of a few minutes on Saipan. From top to bottom, left to right: Corporal Burrell A. Tipton (radio/loader), Private First Class Richard V. Dulin (assistant driver), Private First Class Martin Strand (driver), Private First Class Robert U. Falkenbury (gunner), and Sergeant Robert L. Bodish (tank commander). (NARA)

An observer from the 5th Marine Division assigned to the 2nd Tank Battalion wrote that, in all, only three Japanese tanks were destroyed by B Company, 2nd Tank Battalion that night.

As the Americans progressed north, the 2nd Marine Division approached the ruins of Garapan town. In the late afternoon of June 24, 1944, the 3/2 captured a ridge southeast of the town. At its base was a rock quarry where Japanese had found cover. "The Japanese were down in this rock quarry," recalled Robert U. Falkenbury, gunner in tank C30 C.O.D., the platoon leader's tank of 3rd Platoon, C Company, 2nd Tank Battalion. "There was a rock quarry there on Saipan and I don't know why the Japs was all down in this rock quarry. They [were] just like ants down there … so many of them but they was all confused or something … We pulled up at what we could get to 'em. We just having a field day."

C30 was the only tank in the area in support of Marines from 3/2. "We were just up there on the side … shooting up on them. And there is this road that come up to this rock quarry. Somebody yelled on the phone and told me there is tanks coming up off this road behind us. All we had to do was turn the turret around and I was there waiting for them."

Burrell A. Tipton, the loader/radio operator aboard C.O.D., recalled:

It seems that after the first day's action ashore, our lieutenant [1st Lieutenant Merle L. Severns, 3rd Platoon Leader] could not stand to be closed up inside the tank, so he got out and directed the operation from a phone that was located on the right [rear] side of the tank. The phone had a 50-foot cord. Lt Severns removed his identification, pushed the bill up on his baseball cap, and very few knew him as a tank platoon leader.

When Severns was outside, Sergeant Robert L. Bodish was commanding the tank. Severns had word from the infantry that three Japanese tanks were coming down the road leading to the quarry and communicated it to the buttoned-up tank crew.

The road made a bend where the tank crewmen had an open view of it. "They couldn't see us and we couldn't see them but we knew that they were coming. When they popped around that corner, it was too late then, I already had that sight set on that road. When it come around all I had to do [was to press the trigger]. One shell to a tank." As three enemy tanks appeared, "I fired one armor piercing shell but it was too slow for me … It got all through before it [exploded]." The loader switched to high-explosive rounds into the breech and, "Other shells when you hit a tank it exploded the whole thing. And I hit it and set up all the ammunition on [the] inside because they just seemed like they exploded."

Two Japanese tanks were quickly put out of action. "That last tank when it turn[s] on [the road] … them light tanks they could run fast … How many fast! They saw what was taking place … They had to do something so what he [was] trying to do was hit us and push us over into that rock pit and that way they could stop us." The little Type 95 could not achieve its goal and was blasted point-blank by another high-explosive round. After that, "An infantryman ran up and told the Lieutenant [Severns] that two more tanks were just a short ways over to our left. We moved over to a small tree covered area, and sure enough, there was two more tanks trying to hide," remembered Tipton. "You could track [them] real easy in jungles because they threw so much vegetation down that you just follow the tracks … That way you could follow anybody like that," said Falkenbury. Along with infantrymen, they spotted the two Japanese tanks hiding in the woods and knocked them out.

Falkenbury was awarded a Bronze Star for his actions that day. "I just happened to be at the right place at the right time," he said. Of the five tanks he destroyed, three were Type 95 Ha-Gos and two were Type 97 medium tanks.

The (unknown) crew members of C32 pose with their M4A2 after destroying a Japanese tank south of the town of Garapan. This is a mid-production vehicle, unlike C30, which is a late-production model. (NARA via Morgan Gillard)

This rear view of a knocked-out Ha-Go on Tinian shows the platform used by infantry for riding on the tank. On this vehicle, the platform doubled up as a toolbox. (NARA)

That same day, two more Japanese tanks came out of Garapan from the southern road, charging the Marines' lines. One was disposed of by an SPM, the other by C32, another M4A2 in Falkenbury's platoon.

After Saipan was secured, the Marines headed for the island of Tinian, three miles south. The landing took place on July 24, 1944.

On August 1, the mop-up had moved down the southern island's plateau. For the day's advance, 3rd Platoon, A Company, 2nd Tank Battalion was assigned to L and I companies 3/8 (two tanks to each company). During the advance into cane fields, the tanks destroyed two hidden Type 95 Ha-Gos.

That same day, a section of two tanks from 2nd Platoon, B Company, 2nd Tank Battalion supported E/2/6, temporarily attached to the 3/8 for the drive to the southern cliffs. One M4A2 knocked out an isolated Ha-Go: the 75mm round blew off the turret and exploded the stored ammunition, killing several Japanese infantrymen in the tank's vicinity.

At the end of the day, the island was declared secure, though fighting continued for the next two days.

GUAM

Marines and Army units landed on Guam on July 21, 1944. At 0230hrs the next morning—inland from the southern landing beaches—an urgent call from B/1/4 reached the 2/4 CP. Enemy tanks were heard on the Harmon road, leading to the town of Agat. The 2nd Platoon, Tank Company, 4th Marines, bivouacked near the CP was the nearest tank unit in the area. It was requested to support the Marines who had established a roadblock the previous evening.

Captain Philip C. Morell was commanding the tank company. He recalled:

About two in the morning, coming up Harmon road, they heard mechanized noises. So they called for tanks … of course it was black out, and it's very difficult to move tanks at night, particularly with those periscopes. They didn't have the direct vision cupolas then. [1st Lieutenant James R. Williams Jr, 2nd Platoon Leader, walked ahead and] held up his radium dial wristwatch and led this one tank up to sort of a junction, maybe a trail—on Harmon road.

Lieutenant Williams guided Circle 3 and 4 and placed them on either side of the road. The other three tanks in the platoon, Circle 1, 2, and 5, were emplaced to the left of the road, to protect against flank attacks.

At 0300hrs a column of five Japanese tanks, Type 95s from the 1st Company, 9th Tank Regiment, and accompanying infantry could be heard coming up the road. Marines opened fire with machine guns and bazookas. M4A2s on either side of the road could not see the enemy because of the darkness. Both tanks opened fire with their machine guns and, "when one gunner saw his tracers ricocheting straight up he let a 75 HE [round] go, hitting the first tank, it exploded about twenty yards from his tank," recorded the action report. At the same time, a bazooka team hit that same tank twice with rockets, adding to the explosion. Other Japanese tanks returned fire until "Circle 3 hit two tanks following the first by 10–25 yards—being able to see them by the light of the first tank burning. These tanks also exploded and burned."

American tanks continued to fire at gun flashes, destroying one more Type 95 Ha-Go and dispersing the Japanese infantry. Morell recalled: "The last [Japanese] tank in the column—there was kind of a little bump there—he turned around and started down into this valley. [He] went across the valley and up the other side."

But at dawn, the Type 95 was spotted on Manot Ridge (north of Harmon road). "Circle 2 fired four rounds of 75mm APC, getting two hits which set the tank on fire.

Guam 1944 saw the highest number of clashes between Marine Corps and Japanese tanks of the Pacific War. This is a view of B Company, 3rd Tank Battalion's tank park; a captured Type 95 Ha-Go from the Tank Unit, 29th Division is in the right foreground. (NARA)

The range was measured several days later and found to be 1,840 yards." It was the longest effective tank fire of the Pacific War ever recorded. Morell recalled:

> The Navy flyboys came down and kept bombing the tank—that last tank that was out in front of the front line all day long, claiming to have knocked it off … So [irritated] I got on the channel which I was not supposed to do and said "Hey, You birds! That was knocked out long before you started—Over."

Platoon Leader Williams was awarded the Silver Star for his "tactical ability, cool leadership in the face of enemy attack and courageous devotion to duty" during this action.

On the morning of July 25, 1944, the 1st Provisional Marine Brigade began mopping-up operations at the base of Orote Peninsula. In the 22nd Marines zone, C/1/22 was facing ferocious resistance along the northern shore. Around noon, five Japanese Type 95 Ha-Gos from the 1st Company, 9th Tank Regiment, supported by infantry, attacked on the Piti–Sumay road, parallel to the coastal line.

The Tank Company, 22nd Marines—the former 2nd Separate Tank Company—was in support of 1/22. Informed of the Japanese counterattack, the M4A2s closed in and quickly destroyed the Ha-Gos and dispersed the enemy infantry.

About an hour and a half later, two more Ha-Gos came down the same road. This time, tanks from the 22nd Marines were leading the way. Robert Meier in Triangle 3 Tokyo Rose remembered: "I was watching, there was a road coming up there and I was watching that road. They were coming up the road. And they got pretty close to us up over the hill about 100–130 yards away. I didn't think they would see us." Meier

These two Type 95s were destroyed on the road to Sumay on Orote Peninsula, Guam on July 25, 1944. They belonged to the 1st Company, 9th Tank Regiment, detached from Saipan. (NARA)

had one round in the chamber, ready to go. "We were sat up on top of the hill waiting for the infantry. Two of them [Type 95s] came out toward us and I knocked them out before they even got there … With our 75 … [the] first one I hit in the middle and two guys jumped out of it and ran away … But the other tank I hit, nobody got out of it."

The Japanese tankers did not have a chance to fire back: "they never had this chance. They were moving. They couldn't fire on the move. We could, they couldn't."

That day, the Tank Company, 22nd Marines knocked out a total of seven Japanese Type 95s.[14]

A still from combat footage showing Triangle 3 Tokyo Rose on a dirt road on Guam. Its crew knocked out two Ha-Gos on the road to Sumay. Note the two-tone camouflage. (NARA)

On the 3rd Marine Division's front to the north, one Ha-Go surprised the Americans on the morning of August 2, 1944 by breaking through the lines of the 3/9, north of Tiyan airfield.

The light tank raced down the airfield, chased by two medium tanks from B Company, 3rd Tank Battalion. Captain Bertram A. Yaffe, B Company Commanding Officer, and 1st Lieutenant George R. Cavender, 2nd Platoon Leader, were following the Japanese tank: "We were gaining on the Jap and had our 75mm gun loaded and zeroed on his rear, but we held our fire. We were heading toward our own rear area and there was danger of hitting Marines bivouacked there," recalled Cavender.

At some point, the American tankers lost the Type 95, which had now reached the western part of the airfield. Immobilized in a ditch, the Japanese tank commander opened the turret and fired his pistol on nearby Marines before the whole crew evacuated the disabled tank. Both American tanks finally closed in and destroyed the Ha-Go.

The next afternoon, an armored patrol consisting of A Company and Battalion H&S, 3rd Tank Battalion, one section of the division Reconnaissance Company mounted in two half-tracks, and I/3/21 loaded in six 6x6 trucks, conducted a reconnaissance north of the 21st Marines zone. The convoy was ambushed by Japanese infantry, 75mm guns, and one tank. Fifteen casualties were sustained in American ranks. On the Japanese side, two 75mm guns were destroyed, and an undetermined number of machine-gun nests and infantry were eliminated, as well as the Japanese tank lost to a 75mm HE round.

On the final drive to the north, Marines from the 2/3 were attacked by a combined tank–infantry force coming from Tarague in the early hours of August 9, 1944.

Marines were forced to withdraw into the jungle, but when they returned to the battle site with heavier antitank weapons later that same day, the Japanese tanks had vanished.

14 The official Marine Corps history of World War II credits the tank companies with five more Japanese tanks on August 24, 1944, but none of the unit reports mention it. However, the total number of tank kills by the 22nd Marine tanks on Guam was eight. One might have been destroyed on this date by an M4A2 from the 22nd.

On August 10, 1944, supported by 2nd Platoon, C Company, 3rd Tank Battalion, the 2/3 moved north on the trail to Tarague. One Japanese tank was knocked out by the lead M4A2s. Later on that day, as many as eight more Japanese tanks were found hidden in the bushes on either side of the road. C Company, 3rd Tank Battalion's War Diary recorded: "Only one of the enemy tanks was manned, and it was the first we discovered and hit by our tanks. All others were captured intact. There were both light and medium tanks among those captured."

These Japanese tanks were probably the scattered survivors from the 2nd Company, 9th Tank Regiment and Tank Unit, 29th Division.

PELELIU

On September 15, 1944, the 1st Marine Division attacked Peleliu. Late in the afternoon, after the Americans had established a strong beachhead, the Japanese Tank Company, 14th Infantry Division, supported by riflemen from the 1st Battalion, 2nd Infantry Regiment attacked in two columns at the junction between the 1/5 and 2/1 Marines.

At about 1700hrs, the Japanese tank–infantry team reached the 2/1 line on the southwestern end of the airfield. All Marine weapons were brought to bear on the attackers. A tank platoon from A Company, 1st Tank Battalion was in support and opened fire on the advancing tanks. Coral dust resulting from the heavy American fire drastically reduced visibility. In his tank, Platoon Sergeant James D. Miller could see little outside. As during gunnery practice, he baled out and knelt on the engine deck behind the turret and "exposing himself to intense enemy mortar, artillery and small-arms fire to deliver more accurate fire orders to his crew from the turret of his tank, he contributed in large measure to the destruction of seven Japanese tanks." Wounded during the action, he was awarded the Navy Cross.

Shermans from A Company, 1st Tank Battalion were highly instrumental in repulsing the coordinated Japanese tank–infantry attack against Marine positions at Peleliu airfield on September 15, 1944. (NARA)

Platoon Sergeant James D. Burkhalter Jr found himself in command of a tank platoon after the platoon leader was wounded and evacuated a few hours before. "There were more than 14 of them and only six of us. I didn't think they saw us, so I decided to wait until they got almost on us. I knew that with the element of surprise to help us, our General Shermans would prove more than a match for those Japs," he commented to a reporter. He was credited with the destruction of two Ha-Gos and was awarded a Bronze Star.

Several Type 95s made it down the 5th Marines' lines where other tanks from B Company, 1st Tank Battalion were waiting in the woods south of the airfield. As the Japanese tanks were spotted, the M4A2s "moved out on the airstrip and were shooting as soon as the first Jap tank touched the other side of the airport," wrote Captain Jack R. Munday, B Company commander.[15] Four M4A2s were firing point-blank at the Ha-Gos. The first rounds were armor-piercing and went through the lightly armored Type 95s, exploding outside the tanks. The number of Japanese tanks seriously dwindled when the crews switched to high-explosive rounds.

A tank from B Company joins the melee at Peleliu airfield. Note the track links welded on the glacis and turret sides to increase protection against Japanese antitank fire. (MCHD)

15 Captain Munday was awarded the Silver Star for leading his company during the Japanese tank–infantry counterattack despite a broken arm.

This knocked-out Ha-Go at Peleliu airfield shows the turret Type 97 machine gun installed on its anti-aircraft mount. Several tanks were equipped in this way in the attack against American ground troops on D-Day. Note the fuel drum used to transport infantry during the attack. (Corbis via Getty Images)

Platoon Sergeant Joseph R. Bona in Liz tank number B13 was clearing machine-gun nests on the airfield with the help of B14, the company dozer tank. "[All of a sudden,] six [Ha-Gos] came our way. We hit one with our seventy-five and blew the turret off. That Jap tank bounced 40 yards before exploding," commented Sergeant Glen Mulligan, tank commander in B14.

B13 was also credited with the destruction of one Japanese tank, before one of the Type 95s scored a lucky hit on B13's barrel, putting it temporarily out of commission. It took five hours and 22 hacksaw blades for the crew to cut off 8in. of hardened steel gun tube.

Japanese riflemen were either killed or dispersed about 30 minutes after the beginning of the counterattack when four M4A2s charged onto the airfield. Observing from a vantage point, Lieutenant-Colonel Lewis W. Walt, 5th Marines Executive Officer, reported: "These four tanks played an important role in stopping the enemy tanks and also stopping the supporting infantry, the majority of which started beating a hasty retreat when these Shermans came charging down from the south. They fought a running battle and ended up in the midst of the enemy tanks." In the chaos, one medium tank was even hit three times by bazooka fire from friendly infantry.

After the fight, Lieutenant-Colonel Arthur J. Stuart, the 1st Tank Battalion Commanding Officer, reported: "Thirteen of fifteen counterattacking Japanese light tanks actually attacked our tanks and thus became involved in a tank versus tank action against tanks of four times more power and armor. No attempt was made to avoid our tanks."

Like at Saipan, each Marine participant claimed the destruction of the Japanese light tanks that day. Altogether, nearly 180 Japanese Ha-Gos would have been destroyed if all claims were accepted. Actually, 15 Ha-Gos were knocked out and only two Type 95s escaped the massacre of the Tank Company, 14th Infantry Division but were later destroyed by bazooka teams during the drive to the north of the island.

Tank gunner Corporal Edward E. Brooks claimed the destruction of eight Ha-Gos on D-Day at Peleliu. Some 180 Japanese tanks would have been destroyed, if all tank kills were accepted that day. Note the M4A2 hidden in the bush on the right, in the background. (NARA)

ANALYSIS

The conquest of the Central Pacific islands by American forces turned out to be costly in lives and equipment to both sides.

The capture of Tarawa resulted in the annihilation of the Japanese garrison. Only 17 Japanese and 129 Korean laborers were taken prisoner. The Americans had lost some 1,696 Marines and Navy personnel and were left with 2,101 wounded.

This Type 95 of the Tank Unit, 18th Infantry Regiment was hidden in a sugarcane field when it was destroyed by A Company, 2nd Tank Battalion M4A2s on Tinian. The Ha-Go was no match for the M4 Sherman. (NARA)

The armored units involved in the battle also suffered heavy losses. The American medium tank company lost 12 of its 14 new Shermans. Six were lost to underwater shell holes on the reef, four to enemy antitank guns, one to magnetic mines, and one to friendly mortar fire. This count does not include the tanks that were put out of action at one point in the battle and put back into action. Hence, the damaged Sherman in a duel against a Type 95 is included in the six tanks lost in the water since the vehicle drowned in a shell hole on the beach on D+1. Eight Shermans were permanent losses. A third of the company was either killed or wounded.

Regarding Japanese tank losses, it is difficult to determine the causes since Japanese records are non-existent and no known American records indicate the nature of enemy tank losses. It can however be assumed that most Ha-Go losses were attributed to the action of Marine infantry. A single vehicle was destroyed by a Sherman tank. Of the tank crewmen, a single man was taken prisoner.

The expected Japanese attack on anchored American vessels did materialize in the Gilberts. It was however limited to a sporadic submarine attack on November 24, off Makin Atoll, another island chain in the Gilbert Islands. The escort carrier USS *Liscome Bay* was torpedoed and sank while US Army troops were clearing nearby islands. In total, 644 officers and men were killed. This reminded the Americans of the vulnerability of their fleet and the importance of the rapid seizure of the enemy

By late 1944, the US Marine Corps began converting its tank battalions to the gasoline-powered M4A3. This particular vehicle is one of the eight converted flame tanks, mounting the CB Mk I flame thrower. The weapon's range being limited, its crew replaced the telescopic sight with an additional 30-cal. machine gun on the turret. The photo was taken on Iwo Jima in 1945. (From the collection of Sergeant Major Bert Nave)

islands. Tarawa served as an airbase for US reconnaissance and bombing squadrons until mid-1944.

The capture of the Marshalls was faster than anticipated (completed in less than a month) and, compared to Tarawa, less costly in terms of American lives. The seizure of Eniwetok Atoll cost 339 killed and 757 wounded to the Americans. The Japanese garrison was annihilated as at Tarawa, with only 105 prisoners taken. Six of the nine Ha-Gos from the Tank Unit, 1st Sea-Mobile Brigade were destroyed by American Shermans. Permanent Marine tank losses were four M4A2s from friendly naval gunfire (two M4A2s), enemy suicide attack (one tank), and sinking (one tank).

The battle for the Marianas took the Americans longer because of the larger size of the islands and their value to both sides. Likewise, they were more costly in terms of American lives (6,754 killed and 21,792 wounded). But their strategic value outweighed these statistics. Now, the Japanese Home Islands were within range of American heavy bombers.

Moreover, the Japanese had lost the majority of their airpower over the Philippine Sea during the "Great Marianas Turkey Shoot." Both had a huge impact on Japanese morale.

On Saipan, the vast majority of the 9th Tank Regiment's vehicles were destroyed by Marine infantry weapons: bazookas, antitank guns, and SPMs. The proportion of kills by each weapon is impossible to assess, mainly because of two factors: the first being the chaos created by the size of the uncoordinated Japanese attacks; the second, the time of the day these attacks took place. For example, the June 17 tank–infantry attack occurred at night, when visibility was poor. Several tanks were hit numerous times by different weapons, rendering the statistics even more difficult to establish.

Nonetheless, American official documents credit the Sherman M4A2s with the destruction of nine Japanese tanks on Saipan. The model of knocked-out tanks was, however, not always recorded, making it impossible to determine the exact number of Ha-Gos lost to the Shermans' firepower.

On Tinian, the tank force was entirely made up of Ha-Gos, making the count easier: three Type 95s out of 12 were destroyed by Shermans. American tank losses during the Saipan and Tinian operations are difficult to estimate as well because of incomplete records.

The actions of Marine tanks on Guam were better recorded. Table 7 presents the Marine Corps' tank losses (temporary and permanent) that occurred during the Guam operation. About 50 percent of the losses were credited to enemy action, among which antitank mines and guns were the most important. Only three Shermans were disabled by ambush of enemy medium tanks. Two were knocked out by a Type 97 Shinhoto Chi-Ha, and one by a Chi-Ha at close range. Terrain features were responsible for about 35 percent of the immobilized M4A2s. They were characterized by saltwater entering the vehicles, shell holes, thrown tracks, stumps, mud, and ditches. The rest of the tank losses were due to mechanical failures (<5 percent) and to unknown causes (about 10 percent).

Japanese tank losses on Guam were also better recorded owing to the nature of the Japanese counterattacks during the battle. Rather than the traditional, large uncoordinated tank–infantry attacks, tanks were employed piecemeal by the Japanese. About half of the Japanese tanks were lost to American tank action.

Table 7: Tank losses during the Battle of Guam, July 21–August 10, 1944

	Number of M4A2s knocked out (temporarily or permanently)	Number of Japanese tanks (light and medium) destroyed
Antitank guns	6	0
Suicide teams	3	0
Enemy tanks	3	19
Mines	10	0
Enemy mortar	1	0
Rifle grenade	2	1
Bazooka	0	2
Heavy machine gun	0	1
Terrain features	18	0
Mechanical failures	2	0
Abandoned	0	10
Unknown reasons	?	?

At Peleliu, the change in Japanese strategy resulted in a prolonged bloodbath. As was often the case, only a handful of Japanese surrendered. Many others fought to the death in the deep underground positions they prepared for months prior to the US invasion. Americans suffered heavy losses too—1,336 killed and about 5,450 wounded. But what made Peleliu one of the most controversial campaigns of the war is that it simply could have been avoided. Indeed, US intelligence prior to the assault discovered that the Palaus were empty of enemy ships and planes and that the islands could be isolated and bypassed. But the ongoing preparations for an amphibious assault of this size could no longer be stopped.

As on Saipan, the large Japanese tank–infantry attack that occurred on D-Day led to immense chaos. Nevertheless, the 1st Tank Battalion Shermans were officially credited with the destruction of most of the Ha-Gos that day. A single M4A2 was damaged by a Type 95. Most Shermans were lost to antitank mines during the operation.

The most powerful antitank weapon the Japanese had on hand was the Type 01 47mm gun. But the Japanese had too few of them in the Pacific to hope to hold back the American tanks' advance.

Tankers' casualties were also irregularly recorded, though most American accounts reveal that the great majority of casualties in US tank personnel occurred while men were outside their vehicles. There is no estimate of Japanese tanker losses because only a handful of them survived and no records exist.

The last tank battle where US Marine M4A2s opposed Japanese tanks in the Pacific occurred during the Battle of Iwo Jima in February 1945. Japanese tanks from the 26th Tank Regiment were all dug in, to be used as pillboxes against the advancing enemy. By that time, the Japanese stopped wasting their armored support in futile "banzai attacks." They had realized their tanks were greatly outmatched by American armor and decided that they would be more efficient used as pillboxes.

Thus, the M4A2s of the 3rd Tank Battalion ran into several medium tanks Type 97 and succeeded in destroying them all.

These were some of the last actions of the M4A2s, since the diesel version of the Sherman was slowly being replaced by the gasoline-powered M4A3 within Marine Corps tank battalions.

Also, the use of flame-thrower tanks on Guam and Peleliu, though not completely satisfactory, proved the necessity of developing a better flame-thrower tank to deal with entrenched enemy positions. Thus, for Iwo Jima, the Americans developed M4A3s, whose main armament was replaced by a flame-thrower with a longer range and capacity. Eight such flame tanks were deployed on Iwo Jima and proved invaluable in the capture of the island.

This work has clearly demonstrated the disparity between the Sherman and the Ha-Go, and more generally the tanks the Japanese fielded during the Pacific War. Though their crews were experienced, the technology on hand dated back to the mid-1930s, while American crews benefited from more modern equipment.

Japanese tanks had never been a real threat to the Americans, who enjoyed a wide range of weapons capable of destroying them. The Japanese, however, had too few antitank weapons effective enough to stop a Sherman's progress.

General Mitsuru Ushijima, commanding the Japanese 32nd Army on Okinawa, concluded: "The enemy's power lies in its tanks. It has become obvious that our general battle against the American forces is a battle against their ... tanks."

When the Marianas fell, Japanese defensive doctrine developed a series of in-depth fortifications designed to inflict maximum casualties on the enemy. Here, a Type 97 Shinhoto Chi-Ha, mounting the powerful Type 01 47mm gun, has been emplaced on Iwo Jima. (NMPW)

BIBLIOGRAPHY

Interviews

Bale, Ed interview with Oscar E. Gilbert and Romain Cansière, July 31, 2013

Bryk, Clarence; Edward Bale oral history interview OH00251. National Museum of the Pacific War, Fredericksburg, Texas, September 22, 2001

Falkenbury, Robert interview with Romain Cansière and Oscar E. Gilbert, September 6, 2018

Meier, Robert interview with Romain Cansière, December 4, 2018

Morell, Philip interview with Oscar E. Gilbert, November 5, 1998

Shivetts, Michael E. interview with Oscar E. Gilbert, July 2, 2013

Official reports

Calcutt, Harry, *Special Action Report of Tank Co 22nd Marines on Guam*, March 30, 1945

Calcutt, Harry, *Report on Downside Operations*, February 26, 1944

Gardelle, Lewis, *Observers Report on Forager Operation*, July 13, 1944

McCoy, Charles W., *Special Action Report, Tinian Operation*, August 14, 1944

McCoy, Charles W., *Special Action Report of the Second Tank Battalion*, December 14, 1943

Morell, Philip C., *Special Action Report of Tank Co 4th Marines on Guam*, February 7, 1945

Red Army's Scientific Proving Ground, Department 1, *Report on captured Japanese Tank Mitsubishi built in 1937*, Russia, January–March 1940

Research and Development Division, Directorate of Armoured Fighting Vehicles Production, *Report on Examination of Japanese Light Tank*, Melbourne, Australia, February 1943

Special Action Report, Palau Operation, First Marine Division (Rein), Annex J, Tanks, 1944

Tank Development Board, *Japanese Light Tank – Type 95*, Calcutta, India, June 1944

Articles

CINCPAC—CINCPOA, "Preliminary POW Interrogation Report No.109," *Translations and Interrogations Number 19* (February 14, 1945), pp. 97–108

CINCPAC—CINCPOA, "Special POW Interrogation Report No.113," *Translations and Interrogations Number 20* (February 25, 1945), pp. 103–17

CINCPAC—CINCPOA, "Various Types of Army Radios," *Translations and Interrogations Number 34* (June 27, 1945), pp. 59–62

Books

Alexander, Joseph H., *Utmost Savagery: The Three Days of Tarawa*, Naval Institute Press, Annapolis (1995)

Armored Force Field Manual 17-12 Tank Gunnery, War Department, Washington D.C. (1943)

Chief of Ordnance, *Technical Manual 9-731B Medium Tank M4A2*, War Department, Washington D.C. (1943)

Estes, Kenneth W., *Marines Under Armor: The Marine Corps and the Armored Fighting Vehicle, 1916–2000*, Naval Institute Press, Annapolis (2000)

Estes, Kenneth W., *US Marine Corps Tank Crewman 1941–45*, Warrior 92, Osprey Publishing, Oxford (2005)

Garand, George W., & Strobridge, Truman R., *History of U.S. Marine Corps Operations in World War II, Volume IV, Western Pacific Operations*, Marine Corps Historical Division (1971)

Gilbert, Oscar E., *Marine Tank Battles in the Pacific*, DaCapo Press, Philadelphia (2001)

Gilbert, Oscar E., & Cansière, Romain, *Tanks in Hell, A Marine Corps Tank Company on Tarawa*, Casemate Publishers, Philadelphia (2015)

Hunnicutt, Richard P., *Sherman, A History of the American Medium Tank*, Presidio Press, California (1978)

Military Intelligence Division, *Japanese Ammunition Part IV 25mm-70mm*, War Department, Washington D.C. (July 20, 1945)

Military Intelligence Division, *Japanese Tank and Antitank Warfare*, War Department, Washington D.C. (August 1, 1945)

Rottman, Gordon, & Takizawa, Akira, *World War II Japanese Tank Tactics*, Osprey, Oxford (2008)

Shaw Jr, Henry I., Nalty, Bernard C. & Turnbladh, Edwin T., *History of U.S. Marine Corps Operations in World War II, Volume III, Central Pacific Drive,* Marine Corps Historical Division (1966)

Tipton, Burrell A., *Ours is Not to Question Why, Ours is But to Do or Die*, Dayton Printing Company, Texas (1979)

Zaloga, Steven J., *Japanese Tanks 1939–45*, New Vanguard 137, Osprey Publishing, Oxford (2007)

Zaloga, Steven J., *M4 Sherman vs Type 97 Chi-Ha, The Pacific 1945*, Duel 43, Osprey Publishing, Oxford (2012)

Websites

Oliver Barnham's Ha-Go was restored by Robert Lewszyk and his team in Poland. They published detailed photos of their outstanding restoration work on the page: https://www.facebook.com/Hago-typ-95-Tank-Restoration-Project-1671671063107837/

Akira Takizawa's excellent website dedicated to the history of Japanese tanks from the 1920s to the end of World War II: http://www3.plala.or.jp/takihome/

INDEX